END

Nurturing Healthy Attachment
I wish I had a resource like
give each of my three daug
deserve. Through research, heart, and wisdom, Sorrels and Chalmers
offer insight into why attachment is so important to raising emotionally
secure and spiritually healthy kids."

—John Finch, author of *The Father Effect*

What a gift of practical advice, supported by years of research and
application! Full of hope and promise for every parent.

**—Deniese Dillon, Co-founder and Executive Director Emeritus
of the adoption agency, Dillon International, Inc.**

Barbara and Cathy not only increase your understanding about the
science of attachment, they do a great job explaining different ways to
apply it from infancy, to the teen years, and beyond to improve the
quality of your relationships—and experience a deeper connection with
your children. It's a powerful model of how to love your kids
extravagantly which aligns with scripture and God's love for us.

—Sovann Pen, LPC, MA Pastoral Studies, MA Counseling
SovannPen.com

Nurturing Healthy Attachment is a must-read for all parents who are
looking to establish, strengthen, and rebuild a meaningful relationship
with their children. This unique book provides encouraging and
practical information that's useful for every parent.

**—Alton Carter, pastor and bestselling author of, *The Boy Who
Carried Bricks***

A child's ability to face the future with a strong sense of security,
significance, and strength is determined more by their parents' ability to

maintain on-going and grace-filled heart-connection with them through their childhood than anything else they do.

Kudos to Barbara Sorrels and Cathy Chalmers for showing us how to keep that heart-connection strong and healthy regardless of the age or stage of our child.

—**Dr. Tim Kimmel,** Author of *Grace-Based Parenting* and *Little House on the Freeway*

Much of the relational equity we now enjoy in our family is the result of the principles and applications found in *Nurturing Healthy Attachment.* Great food for thought as you pursue becoming the parent your child deserves, and that God desires!

—**Kirby Andersen, KirbyAndersen.com**

Nurturing Healthy Attachment

Building Parent–Child Connections to Last a Lifetime

Dr. Barbara Sorrels
and
Cathy Chalmers, M.A.

Cover design and editorial by www.MikeLoomis.CO

www.DrBarbaraSorrels.com

www.CathyChalmers.com

Contents

Foreword

Cathy and Barbara take the reader through various stages of childhood from conception to adolescence. They use vivid and helpful examples of what works and what doesn't work in building healthy, life-long attachments.

Nurturing Healthy Attachment is a must-read for parents, and for anyone who has the privilege of being involved in a child's life.

What a gift of practical advice supported by years of research and personal application! So clearly written, this book compels us to look at how we were raised as we raise our own children. It is full of hope and promise for every parent to understand there are methods that actually work to nurture attachment that will last a lifetime.

My excitement kept building as I raced through this book saying, "Yes, Yes, Yes! So glad to know how helpful this book is going to be for all who read and digest this gold mine of information. Many children will benefit from its truths.

My heart was gladdened as I turned each page to another example of how children grow and learn and develop when given the appropriate attention and affection. The connection with how God loves us and how we should love our children is profound and endearing.

— Deniese Dillon, Co-founder and Executive Director Emeritus of the adoption agency, Dillon International, Inc., and the author of: An Inconvenient Calling: A Forty Year Journey in International Adoptions and Humanitarian Aid

Introduction

In addition to many years of friendship, we have much in common—including our professional backgrounds. From fostering healthy child development to treating the effects of trauma in children and families, we both believe the foundational stage of "attachment" is the basis of health for all future relationships.

We love helping parents discover the simple joys of nurturing their children. And most of all, we love being mothers.

This book addresses what we consider to be the most important topic for a parent to understand. Connection, or healthy attachment, is the subject we're most asked about by parents and childcare professionals.

Because we wholeheartedly agree on this topic, the writing of this book is in one voice except in cases relating to a personal experience. Before we begin, here's a bit about us.

I (Barbara) was initially educated in the field of early childhood education, and I later pursued continuing education in neuroscience with an emphasis on the effects of trauma on children. For four decades, I worked in churches, directed childcare centers, and taught in primary school as well as teaching at the university level. Because of my neuroscience training, I now lead a developmental preschool and consult on the subject of trauma in children—training parents, teachers, caseworkers, therapists, and other mental health professionals around the country.

I (Cathy) began my education in the field of psychology and my work in the first psychiatric treatment center for children and adolescents in the United States. This led me to specific work associated with families, adoption, attachment, and permanency placement. I helped cofound an international organization, ATTACh, (*Association for Training on Trauma in the Attachment of Children*), and worked in a developmental pediatric clinic with a treatment team of developmental pediatricians and psychologists. Since then, I've continued to conduct adoption home studies and work in the legal system to secure permanency placements for children, while tackling the complex issues of placements for native children.

We believe an understanding of the basics of child development, and particularly the importance of attachment, will encourage you to follow God's plan for parents to nurture children. We hope this book will challenge you to explore how you were raised, to ask yourself if you were nurtured well, and why you believe what you believe about parenting.

There are many popular misconceptions being touted by "experts," (even Christian ones) and we know an understanding of connection will help clarify your convictions. Child development is amazing and provides us with a glimpse into the mind of our Creator.

Secure attachment used to be commonplace in families, but several societal factors have eroded relationships over generations. Society today has few role models for connection. But there is hope for your family.

We came together with a common interest in children's beginnings, believing secure attachment can shape a child's security in life. Parenting is not for the weak of heart! Parenting is the most challenging yet most rewarding endeavor of your life. God provided a plan to guide us as parents, wonderfully illustrated by the fruit of the Spirit in the Bible book of Galatians.

Love and *joy:* shared in the intimacy of reciprocal connection

Peace: allowing you to rest easy in another's arms

Patience: given by example of calm and thoughtful guidance

Kindness: shared by an attitude of mutual respect

Goodness: coming together and celebrating shared experience

Faithfulness: availability and safety of belonging

Gentleness: through grace-given redirection

Control: of self in recognition of the importance of our child's unique journey to develop and blossom, rooted in a loving parent–child connection

We hope to provide an understanding of the necessary ingredients to grow and develop safe, loving parent–child connections that last a lifetime. These ingredients won't cost you a penny but will promote your well-being and lead to the satisfying family life we all desire.

Relationships are complex, ever-evolving works in process. We offer sound principles, which, when mindfully practiced yield positive

4

interactions between parents and children. When relationships go off the rails, it's important to accurately identify what went awry to properly clarify ways to get back on track.

God's work in our lives bears much fruit when we allow the cultivation of His seeds in our heart.

It's the same with our children. When watered with gentleness, properly weeded with discipline, and tended with trust, our children bear witness to sturdy growth and blossoming. And we reap the eventual harvest of fruit as parents.

Our guidance in pointing to God's leading illuminates the perfect parent–child connection. When you examine your desire to display the fruit of the spirit in parenting, ask yourself these questions:

LOVE: Am I able to parent and devote myself to one who is dependent, without expecting my own needs to be met?

JOY: Am I mindful that joy is an attitude of gratitude and not a situational emotion of the moment?

PEACE: Do I rest in trust that God's plan will be manifested by continual prayerfulness?

PATIENCE: Can I approach situations in a slow and measured manner to more effectively promote the lessons I desire to teach?

KINDNESS: Am I extending the same amount of respect and civility to my child that I would to a trusted friend, colleague, or another adult?

GOODNESS: Do I communicate belief in my child's abilities, encouraging them to give their best?

FAITHFULNESS: Does my child feel the commitment of my time, loyalty, and priority of safety for their well-being?

GENTLENESS: Can I readily admit mistakes and model grace in situations of my own or my child's missteps?

CONTROL: Do I hold myself accountable to meet difficulties only after I approach them in a prayerful manner, with all parties' best interest in mind?

If you can't answer "yes" to all these questions, congratulations—you're human! (That's our professional diagnosis.) We all have room to grow, but once you understand attachment, everything else about parenting falls into place.

As you read this book, you'll remember scenes and feelings from your childhood. Don't push those memories down, no matter how painful. This is an opportunity to heal, and by healing, become a better parent.

Depending on the age of your children, you may read certain passages and experience regret and guilt. For example, whether you have a six-year-old, a teenager, or an adult child, you'll probably see "missed" opportunities to develop connection with your child. Again—welcome to the club. We speak from experience when we say there are no perfect parents.

As you learn more about nurturing healthy attachment, we hope you'll highlight passages that stand out so this book can continue to be a helpful and encouraging resource to your family. We organized the material so you can easily refer to it in various stages of your child's development.

However, we encourage you to read the whole book and not just the parts that pertain to your child's particular age group. Even though you may be parenting a teenager, the chapters on infants and younger children will help you understand the big picture and identify the origins of struggles that your child may currently be experiencing.

An understanding of attachment will help you in all your relationships—as a child, a spouse, a parent, and as a child of God.

Healthy attachment doesn't make a child clingy and codependent; it equips kids to have positive relationships throughout their lifetime. The connected parent–child relationship sets children up for success.

We're cheering you on!

Chapter One

The Roots of Attachment:
The Power of Being Wanted

Before we look at building an attachment relationship with our children, it is important for you to understand *our view* of children. When people talk to us about their child, we listen carefully to discern their underlying attitude in regard to the nature of children. Because what a parent believes about children in general will determine how they parent a child.

Our View of Children
We believe, first of all, that children are a gift from God. Every child is created by an intentional act of God and placed in a family to be valued and cherished. Their value comes not from in and of themselves but from the identity of their Creator.

My grandmother loved to go "antiquing." She and a friend would drive through the countryside of Virginia, stopping at little shops looking for their next treasure. One time, she brought home two lamps that were obviously created out of two ornate vases. Folklore had it that they came out of the first governor's mansion of Virginia. One of them was decorated with delicately painted pictures of angels. Using a magnifying glass, my grandmother was able to decipher a signature in the corner of one of the images as Angela Wolfe.

9

She researched the name of the artist and, supposedly, this woman had paintings in the Louvre museum in Paris. Suddenly, the value of the lamps significantly increased, not because anything about the lamps themselves changed, but their value increased in her mind because of who created them.

So it is with our children. The value and worth of our children lies in the fact that they are created by God Almighty and ultimately belong to Him. They are gifts that are entrusted to us for care and safekeeping. My responsibility as a parent is to be a good steward of this gift and raise them to the best of my ability.

We also believe that children are a blessing and not a burden, inconvenience, or prop to be used for our own selfish interests. In the self-indulgent culture in which we live, there are those who see their children as a financial burden or an inconvenience in their quest for a high-powered career. In these families, children take a back seat to their parent's ambitions. In other families, children are viewed as part of plan to "have it all" with parents overextended, trying to manage the "all," which means too many commitments to adequately nurture their child's needs.

If you battle with a preoccupation with career ambitions, "having it all," or perfectionism in seeing your child as an extension of yourself, this book is a cautionary tale of the effects of those attitudes and lifestyle choices.

One of the richest blessings we receive from our children is a glimpse into the unconditional love that our Heavenly Father has for us. As we love and nurture, we experience—on a small level—the depth of love that God has for us.

As it is in our relationship to God, our daily walk calls us to put aside our daily cares to focus on building our relationship with the One who guides us. It is the same in guiding our children. It's all about relationship.

The Crazy Love of Mom and Dad

Uri Bronfenbrenner, renowned developmental psychologist, once said, "Every child needs to know there is someone who is absolutely crazy about him."

Have you ever marveled at how crazy in love new moms and dads are with their tiny human—who burps, farts, pees, barfs, and poops on them? Not to mention the fact the tiny humans keep us up all hours of the night, make weird noises, and generate piles of laundry. (If we awakened every morning to a burly, unkept, six-foot person who had these same behaviors, we wouldn't find it endearing at all.)

The "crazy love" of a mom or dad is the greatest gift a parent can give a child. It's an unconditional love lavished upon the child just because they are. It's a love that endures the sleepless nights of infancy, the tantrums of toddlerhood, the limit-testing of childhood, and the moodiness of adolescence.

This extravagant love is the essence of attachment, and it's the birthright of every child.

Attachment Parenting

Our approach to parenting is based on knowledge of child development and the developmental milestones that children need in order to grow in healthy ways. When we meet the needs of children at each step, they develop the emotional security necessary to acquire the skills needed to enjoy relationships, play, and learning.

These principles help children meet milestones to accomplish progress to the next stage. The development of trust, which is the first emotional milestone of infancy, allows the toddler to have the security to venture out and explore his world. The courage to explore leads to the toddler's development of autonomy, which means the child comes to the realization that he can make things happen in his life. In that process, he realizes that he has his own opinions, desires, and intentions—which is a beginning of a recognition of a separate "self." We will later discuss associated behaviors and skills that accompany a child in all developmental stages.

Attachment is the basis for trust and the foundational piece on which all further development is built.

There is never a "one size fits all" approach to parenting because every child is different and every situation is different. However, we all need to be aware of and informed about attachment and the implications of our choices.

A common misconception is that we *choose* to be involved in "attachment" or not. The truth is that every parent forms an attachment pattern with their child, whether they want to or not. This is just the way relationships work. By the end of the first year of life, every parent has established a basic attachment pattern with their baby. With this in mind, let's look at the definition of attachment.

11

Definition of Attachment

There are different kinds of attachment relationships, but the optimal one we hope to establish is called "secure attachment." Secure attachment is a deep and enduring emotional bond between a child and an adult who is consistently physically available, who shares a warm reciprocal relationship of intimacy, and assumes responsibility for the well-being of the child.

We all want to be connected to our children. In those first moments of life, we gaze into the face of our newborn and imagine the life we'll have together. The infant gazes back at the face that will offer enduring comfort and ongoing joy and delight throughout the life of the child.

We envision their first word, their first day of school, their first date, or their graduation from high school. We think about their birthdays and celebrations, the good-night hugs and kisses, and joy that we'll share.

No one looks at their newborn and envisions a four-year-old getting kicked out of childcare because of his aggressive behavior, or a sullen ten-year-old who won't talk because he is obsessed with video games, or the rebellious teenager getting his hands on the car keys and wrecking the family car.

We envision a life of connection and the joy that intimate relationships bring. The drive to connect is in our DNA and part of what it means to be made in the image of God. We all long to share a lasting connection with our kids, and they long to share a lasting connection with us.

Sometimes, the biological bond and attachment are confused as the same thing. A biological bond is present at the moment of conception. A secure attachment is a connection that grows as a result of positive and consistent experiences with Mom and Dad.

God has exquisitely designed us in such a way as to jump-start the love relationship between a child and a parent even before we lay eyes on our baby. Some moms report that they have warm fuzzy feelings toward their child the moment they know they are pregnant. Others report that it happens when they see the first ultrasound or feel the first kick. At whatever point the baby becomes a reality, Mom begins to joyfully anticipate the infant's arrival and a mental image of the child begins to unfold—this little person soon to be placed in her arms.

Parents begin to imagine what the baby will look like, what family traits will be passed down, and what they will enjoy doing together. These positive images translate into a positive prenatal environment.

Every emotion a mom feels has a corresponding neurochemical cocktail that is also experienced by the developing child. When a mom carries positive images and looks forward to the birth of her baby, this contributes to a healthy intrauterine environment.

The baby who is joyfully anticipated knows he is wanted the moment he is born. Psychiatrist, Curt Thompson says, "Every child is born looking for someone looking for him." To be wanted and "looked for" is the birthright of every child. On the other hand, there are babies who were a "mistake." The birth control failed. The child was conceived in the context of an extramarital affair, or in a drunken stupor, or as a result of rape. To be unwanted is toxic to the human soul.

Developmental Risk

Sadly, not every child develops a healthy attachment relationship in the first year of life. There are many factors that can undermine the attachment process. Risks to development and developmental delays can occur when there are breaks in—or losses of—attachment. Below are some of the reasons attachment may be compromised, posing risk to the developing child:

1. Unwanted Pregnancy

Attachment begins prenatally. Most moms begin to feel an emotional connection with their baby when they first feel the baby move during pregnancy. Unfortunately, not all pregnancies are welcomed—in too many cases, the baby is only an inconvenience or one more mouth to feed.

2. Congenital birth defects or conditions that interfere with the ability to be comforted by a primary caregiver

Conditions that require an infant be placed in neonatal intensive care can make him too fragile to touch or hold. Touch will over-stimulate the central nervous system and compromise his health.

Medical circumstances are certainly beyond your control, yet there are things you can do to buffer the unfortunate lack of physical touch. Parents can communicate safety and love through other sensory modalities such as singing, softly humming, and "motherese."

13

Motherese is an instinctive quality of speech that is innate to most new mothers. We speak to our babies in a lilting, singsong voice that is higher-pitched than normal conversation. The rhythm, the softness of our voice, and the high-pitched tone evoke a sense of felt safety.

It is common for parents to hold an image in mind of what they think their baby is going to look like. Of course the baby of our imagination is the "perfect" child. Those who are born with birthmarks, congenital deformities, cleft palates, or even the "wrong" gender may suffer rejection at birth. Mom or Dad may show clear preference for a girl or boy, and when the baby is of the opposite gender, there can be a sense of disappointment.

Instead of warmly embracing their baby, parents may turn away. This, of course, is tragic. Because every baby is born looking for someone looking for him (Thompson 2010). For a parent to turn away and not welcome the infant with unrestrained joy and delight is toxic to the infant's soul.

3. Prenatal Exposure to Chemical Substances

For children born to an alcoholic or drug user, exposure to toxic substances in utero may have already altered the brain. Consequently, the child's capacity to engage the world in a typical manner is compromised.

4. Toxic Stress in Utero

It is well established that the emotional state of the mother is communicated to the unborn child through neurochemical processes. The neurochemical makeup of the mother crosses the placenta and interferes with healthy development of the baby. Therefore, moms living in a domestic violence situation, poverty, or highly charged emotional circumstances are unable to have an optimal intrauterine environment.

5. Prematurity

Premature birth is not unusual. For medical reasons affecting both the mom and the baby, prematurity is unavoidable. It can disrupt the attachment process because many preemies are too fragile to be held, rocked, and cuddled. Instead, they are prodded and poked with needles and tubes necessary to keep them alive. The infants, however, have no capacity to understand that the procedures they must endure are actually designed to save their lives. They experience pain, discomfort, and fear at the hands of another human being, and it may "download" into their system as abuse.

6. Difficult Birth

Difficult birth includes fractures or injuries not related to any congenital conditions, and according to The Birth Injury Guide (retrieved 2018) occurs in approximately three percent of live births in the United States. These injuries can occur due to birth weight over eight pounds, births before the 37th week of pregnancy, the mother's pelvis is not the shape or size for a safe delivery, difficult or prolonged labor, or abnormal position of the baby at birth.

A young mom recently recounted the story of her child's birth. After a long and painful labor, it was finally determined her son was breech and for some reason a C-section was not appropriate. When it became clear that her baby was in distress, they pulled him out with forceps. In the process, the pressure of the forceps broke his shoulder, and he was rushed into surgery.

For the next several days, he was in the NICU and couldn't be held or touched due to his painful condition. Even when his medical condition improved to the point that he could be held,, the baby obviously experienced pain. So as any mom would do, this young mother only picked him up to feed and change him and meet his most basic needs.

When her son was five years of age, this young woman began to recognize her child was "different" and didn't seem to have a connection with her. The difficult circumstances of this child's birth likely interrupted the attachment process.

The good news is that the implications of a difficult birth can be compensated through more intensive and intentional awareness and nurture.

7. Neglect

Neglect is the most common factor that undermines attachment. Far more children are neglected than abused, and this takes many forms: emotional, physical, intellectual, educational, and sensory neglect.

There are many reasons people neglect their children. For some parents, it's simply ignorance. We live in a child-illiterate culture. The average person on the street knows little about the brain development of babies, how relationships are formed, or how children learn self-control. For others, overwhelming stress or mental illness can result in child neglect.

8. Abuse
To be harmed by the person who is supposed to love and protect you is psychological poison. Physical or emotional pain triggers the attachment system, and the child's first inclination is to turn to Mom or Dad for comfort and safety. But when Mom or Dad is the perpetrator of the violence, the child is left in a toxic psychological bind.

9. Domestic Violence
It is often a surprise to people to know that domestic violence is even more toxic than outright abuse. The mental health world says it is better to be the victim than the bystander.

Domestic violence is no respecter of social class, religion, or ethnicity. It occurs in well-to-do families and with those living in poverty. In middle or upper-class families, abuse is often a well-kept "secret," but the effects are clearly visible in the child's behavior and approach to the world.

Domestic violence robs children of relationship with both parents and erodes any sense of felt safety. One parent (or parent figure) is the *scary* parent and the other is the *scared* parent who is preoccupied with surviving the abuse. When screaming, yelling, and violent behavior break out in the home, the child isn't going to turn to the violent parent for comfort and security, for obvious reasons. Neither can they turn to the victimized parent because the adult is preoccupied with their own safety and too emotionally unavailable to be a source of comfort and security. The child, therefore, is left psychologically abandoned, which is toxic to healthy emotional development.

10. Removal from Parent's Custody
Be it through guardianship, foster care, or adoptive care, when a child experiences a removal from their family of origin, they experience loss through this break in attachment. Moves are usually preceded by threats to a child's physical and emotional safety and made to serve the best interests of the child.

Permanency is paramount to attachment. If a child doesn't have consistency, predictability, and stability of relationships and routine of daily life, they are constantly left in a state of hypervigilance. Hypervigilance creates a preoccupied state of mind, which leaves them

16

unable to focus on developing the age-appropriate milestones and skills necessary for healthy development.

11. Parental Absence

When parents are called away to take care of extended family health issues, work away from home, or military obligations, it is important to keep the routine and schedule of the children as stable as possible. Phone calls and technology that allows for face-to-face interaction can help maintain consistent communication and buffer the effects of protracted separations.

Your child may have experienced several of the situations described above. We bring these to light because there is hope for you and your child—but only if we address the realities and are willing to offer unconditional love and acceptance.

Unconditional Acceptance

An enormous amount of time and energy in our culture is focused on getting children "ready" for the next phase of development. When I fail to see my child for who he is right now—not what I want him to be next year—I place inappropriate expectations upon him that can result in a discouraged child. If I am truly attuned to my child, I am able to appreciate and enjoy him for who he is in the moment and not constantly push him to "become." I simply allow him to "be."

Inappropriate expectations impair strong connections. When we expect our children to behave or perform at a level that is beyond their developmental capacity, they don't think in terms of, "You goofy adult—what's wrong with you?" They interpret their inability to meet the inappropriate expectations as, "What's wrong with *me?*"

This drive to push our children to "become" has been fueled by the hyper focus on "school readiness." There are programs available to supposedly teach babies and toddlers to read. Tech companies dupe well-meaning but unsuspecting parents into believing they need to buy the latest gadgets so their infants and toddlers will have an edge over the child next door. Parents are manipulated into listening to the latest entrepreneur who wants them to believe he has the best interest of their child at heart, when it's really about his bank account.

When I'm constantly focused on the future and what I want my child to *become*, I'm unable to see and love him for the person he is today. Attunement is undermined, and connections are weakened.

When we only focus on what he is becoming and fail to give him what he needs today, we are likely to miss opportunities to build relationship.

When we give our children what they need today, they will automatically be ready for tomorrow.

Reflections

We all have hopes and dreams for our children. Examine your preparedness for this season of parenting in your life.

What have you allotted for your family in regard to time and resources to focus on this important stage of your lives?

What are your expectations in regard to parenting? What are your spouse's expectations? What are your expectations in regard to your hopes for your child?

How will you communicate their importance and express your "crazy love" to your child today?

Chapter Two

Independence and Attachment: Strength in Connection

I recently listened to a talk show host interview a mom about her new parenting book. The author had three grown children, one of whom was recently killed in Afghanistan while serving as a Navy Seal. She attributed the success of her children to the fact that she raised them to be "strong and independent."

I wasn't surprised by her comment. When I ask parents what attributes they want to see in their children by the time they enter early adulthood, "independence" is usually at the top of the list.

But what do we really mean by this concept? What if the notion that strength comes from independence is an illusion?

Strength comes from connection. A member of any special forces military unit would tell you their strength comes from the fierce loyalty and strong connections they have to one another, to themselves, and to their country. There is camaraderie among these men and women who share similar goals and values. They have the shared experience of enduring some of the most rigorous training in the world, and they rely on each other for their very survival.

Not only are they connected as a team, but these elite individuals are connected to themselves. They know who they are and are aware of their own strengths and weaknesses. They have no illusions as to the limits of their strength, and to overestimate their own capacity would be detrimental to both their own survival and that of their unit. They are willing to lay their life down for our country because of a sense of *connection* to something bigger than themselves.

So it is with all of us. Our strength comes in connection—not independence—and our goal as parents is first and foremost to raise *connected* kids. In fact, we would argue that the root of both physical and mental illness is *disconnection* in the body and mind. Our primary goal as a parent is to grow strong connections with our children that will endure the ups and downs of childhood, adolescence, and beyond.

Strong and resilient children are those who are connected to themselves, to their family, to God, and to the world around them.

Why Is a Secure Attachment Relationship so Important?

1. Advances in neuroscience have discovered that the physical growth and development of the human brain is dependent upon the quality of the relationships and life experiences in the early years of life (Perry & Szalavitz 2010).

This doesn't mean the brain isn't continually developing and connecting. It means the first few years of life present a window of opportunity for the shaping the brain.

The neurons in our brain have little branches called "dendrites" that take in the sights, sounds, tastes, textures, and smells that we experience in the environment. Amazingly, the actual number of dendrites is directly related to the quality of relationships and care a child receives. (Perry & Szalavitz 2010). The structure of a well-nurtured child's brain is more complex than a child who is seriously neglected.

A role of a parent, therefore, could actually be defined as "brain architect."

2. Of concern to every parent is the behavior of their children. A parent's ability to influence the behavior, attitudes, and values of their child is directly related to the strength of the emotional bond that they share. The more connected I am to my children on an emotional level, the greater the likelihood they'll listen to me, respect me, and want to follow my lead.

When parents don't have a relationship of security with their children, they resort to power and control, reward or punishment, and threat and fear in an attempt to make their child comply.

We often receive phone calls from parents when they've hit a wall or have reached a crisis point with their child. The story is pretty familiar: the child has "suddenly" become noncompliant and disrespectful.

Parents are usually surprised when we ask, "Tell me about the relationship with your child. What do you enjoy doing together? What makes them laugh? What makes them afraid? When was the last time you spent one-on-one time with them?"

I spoke with a lovely couple about their seventeen-year-old daughter one evening. She was often staying out past curfew—even sneaking out a few times. Her language was changing, her manner of dress was different, and she was less invested in school.

I know what they were hoping for—they wanted me to give them the magic formula for fixing their teenager and changing her behavior. Instead, I asked them to evaluate where they were in their *relationship* with their daughter and how strongly connected they felt with her.

Both parents were very quiet for a few moments and then began to recount the subtle pulling away from their daughter over the last year.

As her behavior became less compliant and harder to manage, they realized the small ways they began to distance themselves from her. Dad was no longer stopping by her room at night to chat about the day. Mom realized it had been months since they had breakfast together at Starbucks—something they'd enjoyed together through the years—and it had been a long time since they'd gone shopping together.

Both parents realized they had distanced themselves as much as their daughter had withdrawn from them.

Relationships are like putting money in the bank. When we spend meaningful time with our children, connecting on an emotional level, we put deposits in our child's emotional bank account. By meeting the needs of our children with love and respect, we earn the right to speak truth into their lives and have influence.

But, some may say, "Maybe she didn't *deserve* special time with Mom and Dad." It is a mistake to believe that distancing myself from my child in times of noncompliance will change the behavior. But the truth is, when children mess up, they need us the most. We bring them closer instead of pushing them away.

The underlying belief in the statements above is that love and affection are not commodities to be earned. Unconditional acceptance should be freely given. This doesn't mean we don't hold children accountable for their actions. But we do so in a way that doesn't rupture the relationship.

Last year, my husband and I, (Barbara) had a fifteen-year-old foster child live in our home. I quickly learned that she loved to go to Starbucks to enjoy a frappe. We were coming up on a school holiday—one of those teacher in-service days—so the night before, I asked if she wanted to go to Starbucks for breakfast. Of course, she enthusiastically agreed.

When I woke up the next morning and checked my e-mail, a strange screen popped up on my computer. It took me a moment to realize what was happening, but I discovered she got up in the middle of the night and accessed Facebook on my computer.

For obvious reasons, this was not acceptable. I checked the history, and this had occurred at 3:42 a.m. I tracked her browsing history and found no inappropriate sites were visited. Apparently, social media was of great interest to her.

When she came downstairs, I simply said, "Wow you must be really tired!" She whirled around and blurted, "What do you mean? I went to bed at 9:30 last night."

I calmly replied, "Three forty-two a.m. last night." Her eyes grew quite wide. We sat down and had a conversation about the inappropriateness of what she had done, and decided to draw up a written agreement about the use of the computer.

I wrote out some questions for her to think and write about. When are you going to use the computer? How long each day? What sites will you access? Where will you use the computer? What will the consequences be for violating our agreement?

She quickly wrote a beautiful and thoughtful response. There were some answers I couldn't live with, so we came to a mutual agreement on those aspects.

But when we both signed our names to the document, she looked at me with a fearful expression and asked, "Does this mean we don't get to go to Starbucks?"

"Of course not," I replied. "I still want to enjoy our time together."

Going to Starbucks had nothing to do with her egregious use of the computer. To withdraw that promise would communicate, "I don't want to be with you unless you're perfect." Withholding time together would only drive a wedge between us.

It was interesting how our conversation, over a frappe that morning, had a marked "softness" and openness that I attribute to her realization of unconditional acceptance.

This isn't to say the computer problem never occurred again. It did. And the second time, it cost me money, which she had to work off by helping me in the yard and around the house for five dollars an hour until she paid it off.

And we kept enjoying frappes, and conversation, together.

3. Children who enjoy a healthy attachment with at least one parent have a "secure base" from which to venture out into the world. This relationship acts as a fueling station, giving a child the needed emotional resources to approach the world with optimism and confidence.

They aren't afraid to try new things and test their limits. They know when they need reassurance, encouragement, and support. They can approach their attachment figure for the refueling they require.

When their tank is full, they're able to go back out into the world to explore and learn. Securely attached children have an enormous advantage when they enter formal schooling. They're able to invest their energies in learning rather than merely coping. They have an "I can do it" approach to classroom life, which allows them to be fully invested in learning.

This optimistic and confident approach to the world stems from the security of connection. This allows them to exercise independence knowing that safety and security can be relied upon in us as parents. Mental health experts agree that the loss of a secure base is perhaps the most devastating thing that can happen to a child. When children sense danger, threat, uncertainty, and fear, their biological instinct is to turn to their attachment figures for safety and comfort.

They are like a heat-seeking missile—but looking for a safe haven. So when the people who should be their secure base aren't there, it has serious implications. Even worse is a parent who is emotionally or physically abusive to the child. When the person who is supposed to love and protect me is the perpetrator of harm, it is psychological poison.

4. It's within the attachment relationship that children develop an unconscious yet very profound view of themselves that will determine how they approach life and relationships with other people.

At some level, how we feel about ourselves is related to how our earliest caregivers felt about us.

If we were loved and cherished by our parents, we come to view ourselves as lovable and worthy of care. If our earliest caregivers were indifferent, abusive, or rejecting of our needs, we come to see ourselves as somehow flawed and unlovable.

Just last week, I sat with a young woman who experienced emotional and physical abuse by her mother throughout her childhood. With tears pouring down her face she turned to me and said, "What is wrong with me? Why can't my mother love me?"

Children who have positive feelings toward themselves approach other children and adults with positive expectations that they will be accepted and treated kindly by others. They are less likely to put themselves in harmful situations and unhealthy relationships because they believe themselves to be worthy of love and care.

Children who have negative feelings toward themselves approach other relationships and life experiences with the negative expectation that they will be rejected and unaccepted. The unconscious yet powerful belief that they are somehow flawed and unlovable allows them to be drawn into unhealthy relationships. This experience puts them in harm's way both psychologically and physically.

Reflections

As a parent, why is looking at your own attachment important?

While reading this chapter, you may have seen yourself in these pages. Maybe you were the child who was well-loved and nurtured by your parents, and you enjoy the confidence and sense of well-being that early nurture affords. Of course this doesn't mean that you never struggle or have moments of stress and anxiety. But you have the solid foundation that you are worthy of love and care.

On the other hand, you might be the child who experienced rejection, anger, abuse, or indifference. Over the years, you have built up walls, and no one is aware of the pain and self-loathing that you carry inside. No one knows that when you awaken in the night or in those moments between sleep and wakeful consciousness you are plagued with a sense of not being "enough" and wonder what is wrong with you.

A man once told me that he thought about killing himself every day of his life. No one would ever know the self-loathing this man carries. He is accomplished in his field, an involved father, and active in a local

26

church. He said to me, "I've always felt like there was something wrong with me—as if I'm an outsider looking in at the world."

Reflecting upon our own history and becoming aware of the broken pieces of ourselves can be painful yet so valuable as we seek to form healthy attachments with our children. When we fail to recognize and acknowledge our own brokenness, we are unable to clearly see our children for who they are as unique individuals—we will be prone to overlay our own experiences and emotional baggage on our children.

Here are some ways to face your past and nurture your own heart so you can nurture your child.

Finding Forgiveness

Understanding attachment can help us make sense of the roots of our own brokenness. The wounds we carry inside were inflicted at the hands of broken people. It might be our parents, our siblings, our grandparents, or other extended family who were supposed to love and protect us.

It's not about you; it is about them. Coming to the realization that wounded people wound people can set us free to forgive those who are the source of harm. And we believe that forgiveness is key because if we don't forgive, we become prisoners of bitterness and anger, and we repeat the cycle. Forgiveness isn't always instantaneous. Sometimes it's a journey and not a moment in time.

Finding Acceptance

When we view ourselves as fundamentally flawed or "not enough," it is important to embrace our identity in Christ. This is the power of "Jesus loves me, this I know." To know that we have a Heavenly Father who loved us so much He sent His son to die for us is a game changer. We are God's beloved. He loves us with a "crazy love" that's bigger than any earthly father. He wants us to know and experience the depths of His love at the core of our being and with every cell in our body.

Unfortunately, for some, the "church" has been a source of deep hurt and rejection at most vulnerable times. Instead of being embraced and finding the unconditional love and acceptance that Christ would have us extend to one another, some find rejection and condemnation. Churches are made up of broken people. When broken people don't embrace their own brokenness and don't experience the life-changing power of Christ's forgiveness, the tendency is to find fault with others—and ourselves. God accepts you. Will you receive that acceptance?

Finding Community

We all need at least one friend to whom we can make ourselves known without fear of condemnation or rejection—someone who can share our deepest longings, hurts, and desires. They see our worst self and love us anyway, extending the unconditional love of our Heavenly Father.

If you are fortunate, you might even find a small group of people that can function as your own "church." They are people who can accompany you on your journey of self-discovery and healing. You can share your heart and bare your soul with people who love you unconditionally.

Chapter Three

Secure Attachment in Infancy:
The Development of Trust

The development of a secure attachment relationship primarily unfolds over the first two years of life. It's not something that happens in a moment in time.

During the Birthing Process
The birthing process itself plays a critical role in the attachment process. After nine months of living in comfort and security, the baby suddenly feels sensations never before experienced. During delivery, there is enormous pressure bearing down on the baby, which also causes the child to experience pain.

The baby is suddenly thrust out into the world and is immediately confronted with changes in temperature and a cacophony of sights, sounds, smells, tastes, and textures.

Dr. Bruce Perry says the birthing process is the most overwhelming sensory experience a human being ever faces. Never again will we be overwhelmed by so many new and intense stimuli as at the moment of birth.

The typical response at birth for most babies is to cry. In the midst of this bombardment of sensory input, the baby is placed in the arms of Mom, where he experiences for the first time what it's like to find comfort in the arms of a human relationship. The attachment process begins.

The Biological Bond

New moms are biologically different when they give birth. Their level of oxytocin, which is known as the "love hormone," is increased, the effect being an innate drive to love and nurture their child.

The baby has literally been a part of the mom's body for nine months. As a result, newborns recognize Mom by tone of voice and by smell. They show preference for their mom the moment they're born.

Babies also have a biological affinity for faces and, in particular, a fascination with the eyes of humans. We recently spoke with neuroscientist Dr. Warren Finn (Department of Neuroscience, OSU-Tulsa), who researches prenatal development. He discovered that even in utero, the baby has an innate affinity for the human face. When scientists randomly configure LED lights on the abdomen of a pregnant mom in the last trimester of pregnancy, the baby does not turn her face to the lights as observed in a 4-D sonogram. But when they configure the lights to represent two eyes and a nose, the unborn child turns its head to gaze. How amazing is that?

The visual field of a baby is about twelve inches during the first several weeks after birth. This is just about the distance between the crook of Mom's arm to her face. This limited visibility allows the infant to gaze at Mom's face without being distracted by competing visual stimuli. I'm sure many moms reading this book can recall a moment when their babies suddenly became mesmerized by their face.

Dr. Allen Shore speaks of the "maternal gleam." When a mom gazes at her newborn, the pupil of her eye dilates, allowing more light to reflect off the back of the retina. This reflection literally produces the maternal gleam. It's this gleam of light that captures the baby's attention and causes the child to be mesmerized by Mom's face.

What a baby sees in Mom's face during the first weeks and months of life will be the "face" that orients the child to his world. Babies who see a smile and the look of joy and delight know they are loved and wanted. As the infant grows and develops, she will monitor Mom's face to learn what is acceptable behavior and what is not; to know what is safe or not safe; to understand what is important and what is unimportant.

It is our face that will comfort and guide our children throughout life.

There is also a biological synchronicity that happens when Mom rocks her baby. The heartbeat of the child synchronizes with the heartbeat of Mom. When Mom is relaxed and unstressed, her heartbeat is calming to the child. When Mom is stressed out and anxious, her state of anxiety is transferred to her child and the baby becomes ramped up.

But what about dads? What is his role in this process? Dads also experience a drop in testosterone and an increase in oxytocin when he holds his newborn. He is also innately predisposed to love and protect his child.

Babies recognize their dad's voice at birth, *if* he has been consistently present and vocal during the later months of pregnancy. When Dad has been present throughout pregnancy (involved with mother, and therefore the child, in conversation and encouraging talk), the baby will positively recognize and be comforted by father's voice. After birth, his face will also be a source of comfort, as he speaks soothing words to the child.

Conversely, social workers and therapists recount stories of babies being born in the context of domestic violence. Dad abandons the family and never lays eyes on the child after he is born. Months later, he comes back onto the scene. The biological father speaks and the baby begins to cry inconsolably because his voice is associated with chaos and fear.

Dad also plays a huge role in the emotional state of the mom. The best thing a dad can do for his child is to be supportive and emotionally available to his mother. He can strive to create and maintain a stress free environment during the pregnancy and in the earliest months of life.

Sad cases have been told where Dad really didn't want a child and becomes resentful of the time and attention that the baby takes from the relationship with his wife. His resentment adds a significant layer of stress for the mom, which in turn creates stress for the baby. The added layer of anxiety is likely to cause the infant to cry more and be more difficult to soothe, which in turn creates more resentment on the part of the father. And so the cycle continues. Postpartum depression and changing relationships can affect Dad just as much as Mom. Couples need to seek support early on when these changes begin to adversely affect the marital and parenting relationship.

The Building Blocks of Attachment

Infancy is the stage where attachment begins with the interplay of parent and child. So how is attachment formed, and what can I do to promote a healthy, secure attachment with my child?

The responsibilities of a parent that promote healthy attachment and insure the well-being of the child are met in these ways:

- Provide an environment that is predictable. and provide for the child's physical well-being and safety.
- Provide an emotionally safe environment that is encouraging, supportive, and free from humiliation, threat, and fear.
- Support spiritual development and cultural identity.
- Provide guidance and appropriate discipline.
- Promote educational and intellectual development.
- Encourage positive social relationships within and outside the home.

The Communication of Attachment

Secure attachment relationships have some common characteristics that foster security, predictability, and stability for the infant and developing child:

- Physical and emotional availability
- Sensory communication—touch, eye contact, feeding, movement
- Felt safety
- Attunement
- Playful engagement

In this book, we will discuss these building blocks of attachment for each stage of your child's life. All elements remain important throughout their life. But the way in which we exhibit these will be different at every stage.

These components, accomplished over time with intentional effort and attention, build on the foundation started at birth. These fundamental characteristics serve as the connective tissue that keeps us connected to our child through the challenges, losses, and celebrations in life. Our children are then able to hold positive memories of moments of support, comfort, and joy. These shared experiences become the glue that holds us together.

Before children have words, they communicate through their senses. In infancy, intimate communication is exchanged with the parent through sensory channels. Our presence communicated by touch and eye contact, our provision of oral needs through feeding, hearing our voice, and movement that soothes are all sources of communication that allow us to transmit caring to the newborn child.

Does your child feel safe and secure? A child's sense of felt safety is impacted by the availability and attunement of their first and most important relationships.

Being Available

To choose to bring a child into the world is one of the biggest decisions you will ever make. It demands more time, energy, and attention than anything you'll ever do.

To have a child means it's no longer about you.

Meeting the dependency needs of your child is a 24/7 commitment for the next eighteen years. Infants and toddlers are dependent upon the adults in their lives for their very survival. The infant initially needs our physical presence to communicate security. The school-ager begins to visually represent our presence in his mind, even when we are away while he's at school. The teenager holds us in mind for ever-increasing periods as they begin to spend further amounts of time away from the family.

The period of dependency for the human baby is longer than that of any other living creature. They depend on Mom and Dad to feed, comfort, and provide stimulation. They need Mom and Dad to teach them to talk, to know what is safe and not safe, to know how to play, and to know what is important in the world.

In infancy, an emotionally healthy mom will be drawn to her child in such a way that she will feel his needs as if they are her own. She will be compelled to meet his needs, and she finds immense pleasure and satisfaction as she rocks, feeds, cuddles, and caresses her infant—most of the time, anyway.

The baby, in turn, takes great pleasure in her affection and finds physical and emotional satisfaction in their interaction—most of the time. The baby responds by snuggling, smiling, cooing, gazing, and babbling, which in turn rewards Mom's efforts with joy and pleasure. This ever-evolving cycle of the child expressing a need, Mom understanding and responding to the need, and the baby expressing joy and pleasure in her response to his need is the dance of secure relationships.

It's not complicated, but it can feel worrisome. Young moms are often like med students who, while learning the symptoms of rare and threatening diseases, begin to imagine they suffer from each one.

Moms often begin to question their skills as a parent and begin to doubt their efforts to establish healthy attachment. When a mom starts to doubt her ability to parent well, we tell young moms that the litmus test is this: "Do I take great delight in meeting the needs of my baby more often than not?" We all have our moments—typically caused by fatigue—when we are not as responsive as we are at other times. But if we experience feelings of joy and pleasure more often than not, the relationship is typically on a positive course.

On the other hand, there are moms who are uncomfortable, annoyed, or resentful regarding their child's dependency needs. It may be a mom who suffered abuse and neglect as a child and has no role model to know how to respond to a tiny human who is so needy. She feels overwhelmed and inadequate to meet her baby's ongoing demands. Her anger may be covering up a deep sense of fear and inadequacy.

This may be a mom on the fast track to a high-powered career and the neediness of her infant is an inconvenience to her agenda. It may be a mom who lives in poverty and her baby represents one more mouth to feed.

Perhaps the baby is born with a birth defect, and the mom can't let go of the image of the perfect child she was supposed to have. She feels guilty for those moments when she secretly thinks, *This is not what I signed up for.* She may be overwhelmed by caring for an infant with special needs and the inevitable stress that such situations can place upon a marriage.

Some babies are more difficult than others to soothe. Sometimes the joy and pleasure of meeting a baby's needs can be undermined by sheer fatigue. A mom's emotional resource tank can be depleted by endless nights of little sleep. Or, she may have multiple children to care for, with little downtime for rest and relaxation, and her emotional resources bottom out.

Moms must have emotional and logistical support from a spouse, family, and friends. It's important to learn to find small moments all through the day to replenish and restore her own emotional and physical "tank."

Drip Theory

I (Barbara) am a firm believer in the "drip theory." Years ago, in our first house, I bought twenty barberry plants for fifty cents each at a local nursery. They were so cheap was because they were half dead.

I determined I would line my sidewalk with these scraggly bushes and drown them with water to bring them back to life. It worked. But after several years, I noticed a strange phenomenon.

The bushes closest to the house were significantly larger than the ones further away down the sidewalk. It didn't make any sense. We had no sprinkler system, so I watered them by hand, and they all received the same amount of moisture.

I checked the water faucet attached to the front of the house. The ground didn't seem wet, and after staring at the faucet for several minutes I could detect no drips.

Years later, we had some issues with our water line. When the water department came out and opened the manhole to check the water meter, they determined there was a leak somewhere that was ever so slight.

Sure enough, there was a leak at the outdoor faucet that was so small it was undetectable to the casual observer. The tiny droplets of water, over an extended period of time, produced remarkable growth in those nearby plants. I've since learned to use the drip theory in my own life to keep myself sane.

My husband is a quadriplegic, so I had no immediate backup when my children were very young. Not only did I have to manage the dependency needs of my children but also his.

We also had no family in town, so there were times when life was overwhelmingly stressful. I began to apply the drip theory: I looked for small moments all through the day to fill my own tank so I could care for my family.

One of the things I love to do is read. Reading the thoughts and ideas of other people nourishes my soul. When my children were babies, I set a goal to read a chapter a day in a book. Sometimes it was reading a page or two in the bathroom, in the morning before they awakened, or at night when they went to bed.

Sometimes it took forever to get through a book. But slowly, over time, these little droplets of "water" had accumulated into something much bigger. Often I'd have people comment to me, "When do you have time to read so many books?" A page here and a page there amount to many pages over time. It also gave me time to ponder between pages. And these small moments of inspiration, encouragement, and hearing from God were enough to get me through.

There are many reasons that a mom might be uncomfortable or resentful with the dependency needs of her baby. But more often than not, healthy moms take pleasure in meeting the needs of their children.

Here's some good news: the more effectively a parent is able to meet the dependency needs of their child in infancy, the less demanding the child will be later in life.

Sensory Communication

One of the things we find remarkable about attachment is the fact that it develops pre-language. It doesn't come about as a result of the words we speak but largely through who we are.

Experiencing a sense of "felt safety" in the presence of Mom and Dad is essential to the human infant. If we are frightening, our youngest children will recoil and withdraw from us. If we are able to communicate a sense of felt safety, our child will come to see us as a "secure base" and be like a heat-seeking missile, drawing close to find security.

What undermines a baby's sense of felt safety?

- Unpredictable caregivers and unpredictable caregiving
- Chaos and lack of routine
- Basic needs not being met in a timely manner
- Being left alone when in distress
- Loud and harsh sounds
- Being roughly handled
- Intense and hurtful touch

If attachment and a sense of felt safety are not going to happen through the actual words we say, how do we communicate safety to our infants? We communicate with our babies through their senses.

The Power of Touch

Touch is the first language understood by the newborn. The manner in which a baby is handled communicates something about how the infant is valued—or not.

The infant who is cuddled, caressed, rocked, and stroked knows that Mom and Dad take great delight in her. The baby who is diapered, fed, changed, and comforted with gentle, loving hands knows there are people in the world that she can trust to meet her needs.

On the other hand, the baby that is roughly handled or not touched at all receives powerfully negative messages about who he is and his place in the world. Unfortunately, we live in a touch-avoidant culture. Nurturing touch has been subtly undermined by the proliferation of baby "containers" designed for parental convenience.

We call it the "bucket baby syndrome."

The car seat turns into the infant seat, the swing, the high chair, and the stroller. The next time you're in a public setting, take note of how we carry our babies. We carry them at arm's length in a plastic container.

My husband and I were recently in a restaurant lobby waiting for a table. A young couple brought in their "bucket baby" and set him down on the floor in front of them while they took a seat on the bench beside me.

Being a popular restaurant, we waited nearly an hour for a table. The little guy in the bucket was around eight months old. While his parents talked to each other, he cooed, wiggled his arms and legs, smiled, and tried to get the attention of his parents. It was obvious he wanted to be picked up, but the parents were oblivious to his overtures.

We ended up being seated near each other. The parents then proceeded to place their bucket baby on the table, and he remained in his container for the entire dinner. My heart was sad for this little guy.

Fortunately, in recent years, different types of baby slings and carriers have appeared on the market, which allow parents to literally attach the infant to their body. This is a far better way to carry a baby than in a "bucket," as the child still receives the "sensory bath" that is so essential in the first year of life.

Infant massage has also proven to be beneficial for all babies but especially to those who are temperamentally irritable or those who've had a rough start in life due to prematurity, difficult birth, medical trauma, or prenatal substance exposure.

Growth hormones and a cocktail of calming neurochemicals are released through physical touch. Research has found that premature infants who receive infant massage will gain 42 percent more weight and be released from the hospital an average of six days earlier than those without this beneficial form of touch (Field et al 2010). There are many training videos on the market that can teach parents how to do it well.

There's a popular myth in our culture that a baby will be "spoiled" if he is held too much. There is no such thing as holding a baby too much in the first year and a half of life.

Babies spend nine months literally connected to Mom's body. It makes sense that this physical breaking away should be gradual and not abrupt. To find comfort, joy, and pleasure in the arms of human connection is the foundation of mental health and a positive orientation to life.

Babies sometimes want to be held "just because." And that's a great reason to hold your baby, don't you agree?

The Power of Eye Contact

It's been said the eyes are the windows of the soul. Babies are born with a biological predisposition to focus on the faces of those who care for them and, in particular, to focus on the eyes.

Our children see in our eyes how we feel about them. As previously discussed, it is through the "maternal gleam" that babies come to know and experience the feelings of joy and pleasure that they bring to us.

During the first year of life, a large part of the day and night centers around feeding, and making eye contact is a very natural experience all through the day. This is why it's *not* okay to prop a baby's bottle up so they feed in isolation.

Feeding a baby isn't just about the calories and being physically present. Feeding a baby is about the emotional connection that takes place through touch and eye contact. The ordinary act of feeing an infant is a sacred moment and a critical part of the attachment process.

Turning on the television or paying more attention to the phone than your baby undermines healthy emotional connections that are developed by getting to know one another through shared eye contact.

You may be reading these words long after you gave birth, but your voice, your eyes, and your facial expressions are still important tools for connection at any age. We continue to communicate powerful messages through these nonverbal means across our lives.

Feeding and Sleeping Routines

Contrary to popular thought, putting babies on feeding and sleeping schedules isn't appropriate unless there is a clear medical reason to do so. Over the course of the first few weeks and months of life, the baby is adjusting to life outside the womb. Every baby is different and will have fluctuating needs in the first weeks and months of life. Each will eventually develop a fairly predictable schedule of eating and sleeping within the first several months based on individual need. By the end of the first year, infants typically acclimate and assimilate into the daily routines and schedule of the family.

Hunger triggers a stress response in a baby. The hunger pangs in the baby's stomach send messages to the child's brain that all is not well. The baby cries to signal his discomfort and need for help. When Mom responds in a timely manner, the brain and body quickly return to a state of well-being and satisfaction.

When parents don't respond to the hunger cry because they've decided not enough time elapsed between feedings, the child's sense of predictability and emotional safety is compromised. The only thing a child knows at that moment is that he is hungry and in distress, and no one is responding.

The same principles apply to sleeping. There is a lot of bad advice on the internet regarding sleep training. We're led to believe that if our baby isn't sleeping through the night by the time they are four months old, there is something wrong with our parenting skills and our child. Nothing could be further from the truth.

The reality is, these sleep-training programs are more about the convenience of the parents than the well-being of children.

We are told that babies should be allowed to "cry it out—it's the only way they learn to sleep." Parents often give testimonials that they've tried this method and it worked. They let the baby cry it out, and the baby started sleeping through the night.

The fact is, babies will stop crying, but not for the right reasons.

When we let babies cry it out, they eventually realize no one is going to respond, so they give up and stop crying. Again, sleep training will most likely "work," but does the child stop crying because he has given up, or does the child stop crying because they have developed the capacity to "self soothe"? It is critical that a mom knows the difference.

Responding to a baby's cries and meeting their needs in a timely manner, with affection and warmth allows the baby to feel safe and view the world as place where they can count on others to meet their needs.

It's critical for moms to have emotional and logistical support from a spouse, family, and friends—and learn to find small moments all through the day to replenish and restore.

Tone of Voice

Have you noticed that when most people talk to a baby, their tone of voice changes? We don't talk to them like we do the repairman or the clerk in the grocery store. We talk to them using what is called "motherese." Moms and dads are innately driven to talk to babies in a lilting, high-pitched, rhythmic tone. The rhythmic cadence triggers a sense of felt safety in a baby's brain. The power of rhythm to soothe and help children feel safe is well established through research. When we use this soothing tone, sing, or chant to our baby, we create a safe haven.

The Power of Attunement

A baby is so in tune with Mom that when she holds, rocks, and cuddles her infant, the heartbeat of the baby synchronizes with the heartbeat of Mom. The baby also feels her breath, the warmth of her skin, and the vibration of her throat and chest as she speaks.

Not only does attachment involve a biological "attunement" but there's an emotional attunement that grows as well.

The essence of attunement is this: *I see you, I hear you, I understand you.*

Attuned parents feel the emotions of the baby as if they were their own. When the baby cries from hunger, healthy moms feel a sense of urgency to meet the child's need. When the child is startled at a loud noise and begins to cry, the attuned dad feels the child's angst and takes action to comfort the infant.

Attunement is, in a sense, the process of a parent feeling the child's feelings, absorbing those feelings, and reflecting them back to the baby so the baby knows he has been seen, heard, and understood.

Attunement is more than simply mimicking the child's emotional state—it communicates to the child, "I get you. I understand and empathize with what you're feeling." Not only do words affirm the child's distress, but the facial expressions of Mom and Dad will also subtly mimic the facial expressions of the baby.

Parents are a virtual mirror reflecting back to the infant the child's own facial expressions. When the baby grimaces, the parent usually mirrors a slight grimace, interprets the grimace, and says, "Do you need a diaper change?" Assuming that Mom has accurately interpreted the baby's facial expression, the baby knows he's been seen, heard, and understood. The distress of both the mom and the baby is relieved as the baby's needs are met.

Discerning and meeting the needs of an infant in a warm, sensitive, and timely manner is essential to attachment.

When a mom responds with warmth and affection, she communicates to her baby that she takes great delight in meeting her needs. When a mom responds with sensitivity, it means she welcomes and accepts the neediness of her child. When she responds in a timely manner, she validates the child's needs and he learns something about his own value and worth.

Child development experts refer to the "give-and-take" of attunement as the "serve and return" relationship. Much like a tennis player, the baby serves Mom and Dad with a "cue," and they respond in an affectionate, sensitive, and timely way. This seemly simple interaction has profound implications for the baby's growth and development.

Decades of brain research has confirmed the serve-and-return interaction between a parent and a child is what stimulates the brain to make connections. This means that parents are, in a sense, brain architects. The connectivity of the brain and the complexity of connections are directly related to the quality of relationships and interactions in the early life of the child. So when the baby "serves" a smile and a giggle, and Mom "returns" with a playful tickle and grin, the neurons in the child's brain establish connections.

Isn't child development amazing? We are indeed "fearfully and wonderfully" made.

Attuned moms read their baby's cues with increasing accuracy as the relationship grows and emotional connection strengthens. A mom begins to distinguish the hungry cry from the scared cry, and the mad cry from the sleepy cry. This discernment allows moms to respond more quickly and efficiently.

In this ordinary interaction, which takes place over and over throughout infancy, some critical and important understandings are developed within the child that have implications for the rest of his life.

Let's take a look at some of them.

What Attuned Relationships Create

1. Trust

When parents respond to a baby's cry in a timely, sensitive, manner, trust grows in the relationship, and the baby begins to believe the world is a safe place where he can depend upon others to meet his needs.

The security of knowing others can be trusted to meet his needs allows the child to invest his energies in learning about the world and how it works, rather than being preoccupied with unmet needs.

A hungry child can't relax and explore. A frightened infant will withdraw, and the innate drive to master his world will be squelched. A sense of trust that people and relationships are safe enlarges the child's capacity for further relationships.

Children who don't have this fundamental understanding of trust have a reduced capacity to enjoy relationships.

2. Voice

The only power a baby has to get his needs met is by crying. When parents respond to baby's cries, the "voice" of the infant is legitimized. They realize that they can make things happen and beckon others to meet their needs. This is known as a sense of self-efficacy.

As humans, we are born to have influence in our world. We are not created to be helpless and at the mercy of the people and forces around us. When we respond to our baby's cries, we acknowledge and reinforce his sense of self-efficacy and the fact that he is powerful enough to get his needs met.

When parents fail to respond to an infant's cry, the baby begins to realize his voice has no power. Over time, his voice will be silenced. The baby will realize it's not worth crying because no one will respond.

In extreme cases, these infants will become silent weepers. They literally stop crying, but their face and body look as if they are crying. This isn't uncommon when babies are warehoused in understaffed orphanages.

In less extreme cases, the infant internalizes his needs and "checks out." He comes to understand he either has to ignore his own needs or take care of himself. When children whose voice has been silenced get older, they develop survival strategies usually labeled as "dysfunctional."

The toddler who can't count on parents to respond to his hunger either hoards or gorges when food is available to compensate for the uncertainty and unpredictability. The child whose cries are ignored will develop manipulative behaviors to receive the attention of adults in an attempt to get their needs met.

3. Cause and effect

The brain is an association-making machine. It's constantly making connections *between* events and outcomes. When a baby cries and Mom and Dad respond in a timely and sensitive manner, a connection is made in the baby's brain that says, "When I express a need, Mom and Dad respond." Cause-and-effect thinking is the foundation to morality. When I do *this*, the expected outcome is *this*.

When our response to our baby is inconsistent, these basic associations can't be made. They will struggle with this fundamental way of thinking. They will be unable to understand the implications of their behavior. As they get older, this becomes a problem when they are learning how to be a friend and make a friend.

Without cause-and-effect thinking, they are unable to make simple connections between their behavior and the response of others. *When I'm kind to other people, they're likely to be kind to me. When I hit someone, I'm likely to be hit in return.*

4. Secure Base

Perhaps the most important benefit of a secure attachment relationship is the fact that the child has a "secure base" from which to venture out into the world. The knowledge that there is a warm, responsive adult who is consistently available to meet the needs of the child allows him to venture out into the world with curiosity, courage, and optimism. His emotional and psychological energies can be invested in learning about the world and how it works rather than merely coping. As the child enters the world of school, they are able to fully engage and make the most of opportunities to learn and grow. Mental health experts agree that the absence of a secure base is the single most detrimental challenge a child can face.

Playful Engagement

Not only do we respond to the basic needs of infants to ensure their survival, we also respond to their social need to play. First-time parents often think they're going to bring the "Gerber Baby" home from the hospital. But instead, they bring home a wrinkled, puffy-eyed, tiny human who sleeps all the time.

But around four months of age, the social nature of the child begins to blossom and the Gerber Baby suddenly appears. The infant begins to smile and coo at Mom. With eyes wide open, arm and legs wiggling and flailing, babies communicate, "Come play with me!" "Take delight in me!" Mom reads her baby's signals to engage and may respond by playing Peek-a-Boo or with playful tickling.

Responding to a baby's invitation to play is as important as responding to hunger, discomfort, and fear. The baby learns to find joy and pleasure in human relationships. Playing simple games such as Peek-a-Boo and Pat-a-Cake strengthen the emotional connection between a parent and a child. In these simple moments of pleasure and joyful interaction, babies begin to develop a basic understanding of turn-taking and the give-and-take of social interaction.

Practical Tips for Parents of Infants:

Availability

Consciously free yourself of work concerns or other preoccupations when engaging with your baby. Drink in the experience, and focus on the sensory connections you have with your child—how they mold when held, their response to your talk, facial expression, and tone of voice.

Felt Safety

Concentrate on feeling your baby in your arms. Feel your tension leave as you focus on your body and how you support and communicate safety and relaxation to your child. Rhythmic movement is often helpful to relax your infant. Note the individual preference of your child's process of relaxation.

Attunement

Note your child's emotions and how they are communicated. Note differences in hunger reactions vs. wanting to be changed, or seeking comfort. When you can identify your child's personal expression of needs, let them know you understand: facially, verbally, and gently. This is how trust is born.

Playful Engagement

Practice communicating emotions of delight through tone of voice, facial expressions, and touch that encourages your infant in play. Watch as your little one mirrors your facial expression! Little Piggies (with toes) and Itsy-Bitsy Spider (with fingers) are terrific games to play with infants.

Reflections

As you read about the needs of children, do you recognize your own God-given needs? They don't disappear as we become adults. As you get in touch with the needs that originate for all of us in infancy, look within and ask yourself, "How am I getting each of these needs met in my own life?" Are you getting your own quota of touch, meaningful time spent with eyes focused on you, and play in your life? Are you being heard by someone who finds delight in being attuned to you?

Apply each of the sensory needs we develop as infants to your own experience. It is important that parents take time in relationship with one another. Respite times for relaxation—and efforts to recognize both your individual needs and needs as a couple—are essential. We often forget or feel too busy as new parents to take the necessary time to refuel. By doing so, we can be available to ourselves for self-care, as well as to our marriage, which continues to need nurture after the birth of our children. These as well as other relationships give our lives meaning.

Upon the birth of a child, self-care is one of the things most new parents surrender. It's true that our priority has shifted as we make way for a new season of life when the focus becomes another. But in this season of life, appropriate self-care has never been more important. Many parents successfully share childcare time in order to allow their partner to take a much-needed break—to take a walk, talk with a friend, or simply have alone time to think and relax.

Time spent together to nurture your marriage is important as well. In the midst of a great life transition, time together to celebrate life's blessings is also an investment in your entire family. Intense emotions are at play during this time, and having a date night to track your adjustment is important to a healthy marriage.

How can you apply the drip theory to your everyday life? What fills your tank? Are you making time for a few drops of water throughout your day?

Chapter Four

Attachment Patterns:
The Interplay of Parent–Child Relationships

By the end of the first year of life, a baby has an identifiable attachment pattern or "template" that tells him what to expect from relationships. When the child receives warm and responsive care from Mom and Dad, he expects to receive the same from childcare providers, extended family, and others with whom he comes in contact. Mom and Dad meet his needs for intimacy in a warm and consistent manner. His needs are met by those whose voice, smell, and touch are familiar. This has served to relay the beginnings of a primary relationship with his mother.

If the needs of his mother have been met during her pregnancy and she has maintained a stable emotional life, the child will be the beneficiary of the same experience. He will comfortably transition from the warmth of the womb to the new and expanded environment of a home life with additional sights, sounds, and stimulation.

In contrast, if his mother has been exposed to a harsh and unpredictable pregnancy, with little support or resources to nurture his intrauterine development, he will transition into the world with the experience and expectation of negative interactions. It will be difficult for this child to enjoy a state of calmness and sense of well-being due to the adverse impact on his regulatory system.

A child who is adopted or fostered at birth has suffered a rupture of the biological bond. It is experienced as a loss of all that is familiar. It is important to recognize this truth and provide intense and intentional focus on nurture and security. This initial loss is significant and requires a greater degree of felt safety, availability, sensory communication, playful engagement, and attunement.

As the needs of the infant become more directly experienced by the mother and father, care becomes increasingly demanding. If the parents are well resourced with preparation, education, and support and have created an environment of emotional and physical stability, the child will develop a sense of security and healthy attachment. On the other hand, a child born into an inconsistent, unpredictable, and unprepared home environment will be insecure in his approach to the world and fail to develop secure attachment relationships.

Parents who are ill-equipped to meet the dependency needs of children are likely to be overwhelmed with the 24/7 demands of infants who are unable to care for themselves. When parents expect babies to immediately reciprocate their love and affection, they may become disillusioned and disappointed with their infants. This sets the stage for unrealistic expectations, which can lead to unhealthy attachment patterns. The danger is we unconsciously absorb our parents' feelings and attitudes toward us and carry those feelings around for the rest of our lives.

Seventy percent of us will maintain the same attachment pattern we had at one year of age and reproduce that same pattern with our own children. Our initial parent child interactions affect our approach to all future relationships. The type of attachment relationship we experience has a ripple effect on all aspects of development and across future generations. This is why healthy attachment is so critical.

There are four types of attachment patterns, and each describes a different kind of attachment that characterizes the parent–child relationship.

1. Secure Attachment
Secure attachment is fostered by a parent who maintains emotional balance and provides for their infant a calm and stable environment that prepares them for the challenges of the world beyond the home. Attuned parents accurately read the sensory cues of the infant and respond in a way that makes sense to the child. For example, a child turns his head away when mom is attempting to give him a

spoonful of applesauce. But Mom insists that the baby needs to eat it all. She continues to prod and poke until the baby finally screams in protest. Consequently, mealtimes were inevitably unpleasant. On the other hand, Mom recognizes the turning of the head as the baby's way of saying they have had enough. She respects the child's cues, follows his lead, and doesn't try to cajole, bribe, or force the baby to eat more. The attuned mom and baby are able to enter into a reciprocal dance of nonverbal communication and respect for one another's needs.

Nurturing parents can adapt to increasing demands of the infant because they have structured their lives to make this experience a priority. Securely attached children typically have attuned parents who have a reasonable degree of emotional strength and maturity. They limit their obligations, conserve their energies and efforts to provide the infant with consistency of food, attention, and availability. The parents respond quickly and warmly to the child's distress and basic needs with a gentle touch and soothing voice. This communicates to the infant a sense of security and comfort that allows the infant to truly rest without undue attention to outside stimulation.

When an infant experiences the full attention of their parent and bathes in all the sensory delights of sight, sound, and movement, he begins to function within the comfort of consistency, stability, and predictability. Even though parenting an infant is a demanding task, these parents find great pleasure and joy in meeting the needs of their child. Playful interactions become a normal and regular part of the relationship, and mutual delight between parent and child is obvious.

The child has developed a "secure base" of trust that then allows the child to feel safe to explore as he makes his way through the developmental tasks of infancy. Exploration is the flip side of attachment. Using his parents as a secure base, the toddler ventures out, stopping to look back or return to be refueled for the next foray away from his nurturing parent. As soon as he has wandered too far, has experienced fear, or has been startled, he quickly returns to the safe haven of his parent, seeking physical closeness. This safety, exploration, and seeking of physical proximity to an available attachment figure are the hallmarks of secure attachment.

Children with secure attachments approach the world with an overall sense of hope and curiosity. They are pleasant to be around and have an internal sense that they are enjoyable and worthy of care. They get along with other children, respond well to appropriate adult authority, accept comfort from others when hurt or upset, and enjoy exploring the world and trying new things.

When they enter school, their energies can be invested in learning rather than merely coping, because they have an inner sense of security and belief that the world is a safe place.

That isn't to say securely attached children don't have their moments—they do. But they quickly recover from momentary discord and get back on track to enjoy life and relationships. They trust others will act in their best interest. The security afforded a child who is securely attached paves the road for future pursuits, as these children aren't preoccupied with having to attend to factors outside themselves, either from sensory distractions or relational distress.

If an older child is not demonstrating attachment security, it is important to meet them at the developmental stage in which they are functioning. Attention to building sensory comforts through holding, rocking, eye contact, and the building blocks of earlier attachment need to be tended to meet those former dependency needs.

The next two styles of attachment focus on insecurity expressed in two ways: preoccupied or anxious parenting and ambivalent or avoidant parenting.

2. Insecure Anxious and Ambivalent Attachment

When parents haven't received warm, loving attention as infants, it is sometimes hard to know what emotional support to give to their child.

In looking back at how you were parented, it is important to understand your personal history, in view of: your parents' availability, having your feelings respected, and means of comfort given you by touch, sight, and sound. Were your parents available to you or involved in other pursuits such that you were to be "seen but not heard"? Were they able to provide encouraging words and sensitive touch when you were in need?

It is important to understand that those who parent from an insecure position are not bad people. They're typically people who are overwhelmed by life and simply don't have the resources to cope. They genuinely love their kids, but they don't have the emotional resources to provide consistent nurture and care. They are often overwhelmed by finances, health issues, or other life stressors. They have the best of intentions but are unable to provide the consistency of care required by babies and young children.

Parents with an anxious and ambivalent attachment style tend to be unsure of how to parent, and instead of being a calming source of balance and equilibrium for a baby's upset, they tend to absorb the baby's anxiety. This parent may become stressed and rattled to the point that they are unable to deliver comfort and meet the infant's needs.

Insecure parenting is observed in those who are preoccupied to the point that they are unable to reliably respond to their children. Parents may show a lack of interest because they are so involved in their own lives they may miss vital cues to attune to their child's needs. They may be thinking of other things—a business meeting, obligation, or activity—instead of focusing their attention on the here and now. They are unable to accurately see, hear, and understand their child in the moment. As a result, they will be unable to read their child's needs.

For example, a five-year-old girl in Daddy's arms tries to get her father's attention while he's looking at his cell phone. Dad doesn't notice his daughter's bid for attention until his child physically pulls his chin toward her in order to get him to look into her eyes.

These parents may be so preoccupied that they fail to notice instances when their child needs their protection, yet be over-protective and impose limits that are inappropriate based on the child's need. A lack of attunement can result in the parent sending mixed messages that are confusing to the child.

Preoccupied parents are out of sync with their children's needs and are likely to impose their own interpretation of a particular situation and respond out of their own needs rather than to the need of the child.

Another common example: Mom lets her young child repeatedly run down a steep hill with no supervision but doesn't let her child play on the age-appropriate playground equipment because she is on the phone with a friend.

The neediness of the parent can sometimes result in a role reversal whereby the parent expects the child to meet the parent's emotional needs. The child is expected to provide reassurance and support to the anxious adult. This reversal of roles leaves the child feeling unprotected and unsure of how to fulfill Mom's expectations and needs.

For example, a four-year-old becomes Mom's confidant in regard to a messy divorce situation. Mom has no friends and expects her child to fill this void. The child bears emotional and psychological burdens she is unprepared to carry.

The unpredictable behavior of the ambivalent parents sets up unreliable protection for the child, leaving him feeling anxious in response. Sometimes the parent responds quickly with warmth and affection and, at other times, with anger and irritability. Or, they may not respond at all.

The uncertainty of response can lead to the child using exaggerated emotion to manipulate parents to get what they want. Feelings are often exaggerated because they're never quite certain parents will take note of their distress, and intense emotions are certain to get the parent's attention. As children get older, they may resort to temper tantrums or attention-seeking behaviors.

Children with insecure anxious attachment can be both demanding and clingy. They are difficult to satisfy—nothing is ever quite right. In times of conflict, they may escalate the situation to maintain control and keep the attention of the adult.

The small child hits his head on the table and while he's crying, Mommy frantically says, "Tell me you're okay, tell me you're okay!"

The four year-old is left to get his own breakfast.

The request for school supplies by the third grader is ignored for days while the child suffers the embarrassment of not being prepared for school.

Children who have been insecurely and anxiously parented struggle in relationships with others. They are uncomfortable with intimacy and closeness and give the impression they can take care of themselves. They live life in their heads rather than being connected with others at an emotional level.

The six-year-old playing with a friend keeps wondering when Mommy is coming back. His friend keeps trying to get him to focus on the trucks they are playing with, but the six-year-old fears being abandoned, is unable to give attention to playing with his friend, and worries, *When will she be back? Will she leave me here?*

The insecure ambivalent child struggles to fully engage with his peers. He is so preoccupied and anxious that he is unable to enjoy relationships with others. His need to control the attention of adults leaves him unable to relax and fully participate in play. He constantly gets interrupted by his lack of being able to focus on his connection with another. He is unsure of what will come next, is unable to read the cues of his friend, and vacillates between feeling anxious and angry. His response is unfocused and nervous, due to his feelings of anxiety and emotional uncertainty.

This is the result of the child whose parents have not been attuned to his needs for comfort and fear. They are often parents who want to avoid the anxiety of separations and leave the child without warning or the memory of an affectionate goodbye. They sneak out under the pretense of not wanting to upset the child, but the real concern is their own angst or wanting to hurry up and get on with their day.

Research indicates some other interesting tendencies as well.

Insecure, anxious children are more likely to become addicted to substances later in life than children with other forms of attachment are, and they're more likely to become victims of bullying behavior. Insecure in their relationships with others, they self-medicate to ease their lack of social skills and often let others take advantage of them, unsure of how to navigate secure relationships of give-and-take.

Anxiously attached babies cry more at one year of age than other children and can be difficult to soothe. As babies, their "voice" was often ignored, so they resort to other forms of manipulation to get what they want.

Insecure, Dismissive, and Avoidant Attachment

The parent who displays an avoidant or dismissive style of attachment is likely to be a parent who demands compliance from, and exerts control and authority over, a child. They may be somewhat rigid and require unreasonably high expectations of their children. Focused on their own standards of acceptable emotion and behavior, they tend to be unable or unwilling to accept the cues the young child exhibits.

For example, a mother ends her seven-year-old's play date abruptly and without warning. She demands, "Pick up these toys and clean up this room. We've got to go now!" By dismissing her son's need for closure, her interaction is likely to evoke an aggressive protest from her child.

Her dismissive response gives the child no advance warning that soon they must leave, and prevents him from bringing some positive closure to a fun time had with a friend. Avoidant parents exhibit no attunement to the child's need end an activity with a sense of positive feeling and successful social skill mastery.

These parents may read their child's needy behavior as manipulative or not to be tolerated. They desire for their children to be and act more "grown up," thinking their world to be silly and something to be rapidly "grown past." Insecure/dismissed children are typically raised in homes where the interaction between parent and child is characterized by harshness and irritability. The neediness of their children overwhelms the parent, and they respond with anger and frustration. Sometimes these parents are dealing with mental illness, addiction, or clinical depression. Catastrophic illness or injury, poverty, or other trauma may also be the source of overwhelming stress.

The dismissive parent may be a single mom who is struggling to survive emotionally and financially—or a father who's trying to deal with a mentally ill wife and two small children. These parents rarely if ever have a support system to encourage them in life's struggles.

Dismissive and avoidant parents may fail to protect their children and allow them to take unnecessary risks. This reinforces their views that growth is achieved through action, regardless of readiness. They view themselves as tough in their parenting and compliance is valued as positive, with little regard to their child's "voice." They don't take the time to nurture their child with encouragement or teach skills progressively, building skill development at the child's pace. Instead, they issue commands to be followed.

Children parented by dismissive and avoidant parents may develop two types of avoidant behavior: "aggressive avoidant" or "withdrawn avoidant."

The "aggressively avoidant" child views intimacy as a threat, and they respond with anger and pushback. At times, these children may seem to take delight in the discomfort or pain of others. This may be the child who avoids eye contact, who may find more pleasure in things rather than people, and who rarely seeks out comfort from others when they're hurt. They can be sullen, oppositional, and ignore requests from parents. They're unable to express empathy toward others because they haven't experienced empathetic care.

Johnny is a preschooler who belittles his playmates. He is always the last to line up on the playground, ignoring the reminders from his teachers. With other children, he brags about being the best at activities and points out the inabilities of other children to complete activities as well as he can. He makes fun of their artwork. Avoidant children mask their insecurity with bravado and an inflated view of self at the expense of others.

The "withdrawn avoidant" child tries to fly below the radar and be perfect so as not to draw attention to himself. He has learned that attention may elicit an angry or harsh response; to avoid these uncomfortable interactions, he withdraws and isolates himself. Often, these children are regarded as "perfect" children because they require so little time and attention from parents and caregivers.

Both the aggressive avoidant and the withdrawn avoidant are Lone Rangers, and their journey through life is often characterized by alienation, isolation, and self-protection.

Research indicates that by the time these children are in middle to late elementary school, they can become the school bullies. They have little empathy for others because their parents were unable to show them empathetic care.

The avoidant child can be prone to sudden and violent emotional outbursts. Outwardly, they may seem cool, calm, and collected most of the time, but strong emotions simmer below the surface. A seemingly small incident may trigger a violent or extreme response.

Insecurely dismissive and avoidant children are typically raised in homes where the interaction between parent and child is characterized by harshness and irritability.

There is yet another dynamic in the homes of our modern culture that creates avoidant relationships. That dynamic involves materialism that can masquerade as success.

Mom and Dad are on the fast track to high-powered careers. They bring children into the mix simply because it's the expected thing to do. Nurturing their children is inconvenient and gets in the way of their lifestyle and their career. They gladly pay others to care for their children and meet their needs. The neediness of their kids is a source of irritation.

Outwardly, these children appear to have everything they need: designer clothes, every toy and gadget on the market. They are provided lessons in everything from tennis to voice to piano and martial arts. They attend the best private schools, but these children are often lacking genuine warmth and connection to their parents.

It's a sad indictment on our current society.

There's a Chinese proverb that says, "The best time to plant a tree is twenty years ago. But the next best time to plant a tree is today." You may be seeing aspects of your parenting that could foster insecure or avoidant behavior. But you can still apply what you're learning from this book with your children.

It may take more grace, patience, and determination the older your child becomes, but never stop nurturing your child.

Put down your smartphone, and turn off the TV. Begin to see who your child is and what their needs might be at that moment. Honestly assess your own style of attachment and attune yourself to your child in an unhurried way. Provide your child with the security, nurturing, and soft words of encouragement they crave. Have regular fun together; get out the toys, and make a habit of family game nights!

Disorganized Attachment

Parents who display a disorganized attachment style are often those parents whose children are most at risk for abuse or neglect. Many of these parents have backgrounds of abuse and neglect. They haven't acquired the necessary skills to develop patience or empathy. They are unable to tolerate and manage their own frustration and stress.

They may be punitive in discipline and use shaming in efforts to bring about behavioral and emotional control with their child. Rejecting language and threats of abandonment may also be used when under stress. They may use fear as an attempt to change behavior and this, combined with inconsistent expressions of love, leave the child with mixed messages and confusion.

Usually self-absorbed, these parents may leave their children with others for increasingly longer periods of time. When with their children, they often expose them to risky behaviors, discuss or view inappropriate material in their presence, and fail to protect them. There is little to no attunement to the child's needs, with little limit-setting or structure given to meet the child's needs for consistency. These children may be subjected to unpredictable and unstable moods and behavior. Left to adapt to these circumstances, children's emotions bounce among anxiety, fear, and anger, leaving them in a constant state of stress and unable to maintain a stable balance of emotion.

The child with disorganized attachment will demonstrate characteristics of both the avoidant and ambivalently attached child, and this pattern is most associated with abuse. These kids will be very unpredictable and respond in different ways to different experiences. They learn early on that concern for their welfare can't be trusted to the adults in charge. These children tend to be nervous and experience stomachaches, headaches, and other physical complaints related to stress. They're subjected to heightened levels of stimulation, living with the unpredictable behavior and emotion of their parents, who keep them highly vigilant and preoccupied. This overpowers their physical and emotional ability to cope, and gradually, even smaller threats will bring about the same overwhelming emotional response, as the brain sounds the alarm to self-protect.

These children protect their hearts by taking on increasing control, with this self-protection exhibited by "rejecting others before they have an opportunity to be rejected." This self-protection is often confused with opposition.

If children struggle with these issues because of adoption, multiple foster placements, or numerous losses of relationship, it is important to understand the child's need for increased structure at home and school. They thrive best in environments that are predictable and ordered around consistent routine. Transitions are a challenge, and they will require a great deal of patience and support to navigate them well.

The disorganized child has been exposed to what Penelope Leach (2018) calls "scaregiving." The fearful settings in which they've been raised create an extreme level of anxiety and need to control their environment. This can manifest in rigidity of behavior and thinking, and an inability to flexibly manage ordinary challenges of daily living.

Foster and adoptive parents need to realize this: what the disorganized child fears the most is your love. It is common for these children to reject those who extend love and acceptance because their history has told them that people aren't to be trusted. Therefore, parents should not take their rejection personally as they are simply bumping up against the child's history.

It may be necessary to seek mental health treatment to support the family's process of healing. Nothing can shortcut the child's process toward trust. Intentional, patient, and persistent stability of routine, emotional guidance, and in many cases outside therapeutic resources, may be necessary over the long haul with these children. Sometimes, love alone is not enough.

Reactive Attachment Disorder

Children diagnosed with severe attachment disorders typically suffer from extreme abuse and neglect early in life. Attachment occurs on a continuum from a child being securely attached in relationship to their parents, to being severely disordered—not able to form or consistently maintain security in relationships.

Children who have been parented at the extreme end of a disorganized attachment style are in the greatest need. This can prevent them from forming trust with another human being. These children are often diagnosed with Reactive Attachment Disorder, typically suffering chronic and extreme abuse or deprivation early in life. Extreme abuse can be overwhelmingly detrimental to the mind, body, and soul, and as debilitating as any chronic disease. Abuse can change us physiologically as well as emotionally.

Too often, these children have no feelings of hope, no sense of self-worth, or no comprehension of human affection. Sometimes children with Reactive Attachment Disorder are adopted into loving, well-adjusted families, but their adoptive parents soon realize love is not enough. Parenting a child with extreme attachment disorder requires specialized knowledge, training, and commitment.

Research by Purvis and Cross has demonstrated that healing can and does happen, and there is enormous reason for hope. They note the ingredients in healing children with complex trauma. They include the following:

• Empowering the child by providing a foundation of safety in their lives

• Connection to healing and secure relationships

• Correction of ineffective behavior patterns and development of effective coping and self-regulating behavior

Parents of children with attachment disorders need an understanding of attachment, a neurological perspective of brain development under stress, extreme patience, and access to resources. These, along with heightened self-care and accessible support systems, will help to effectively parent.

While this can be daunting, for parents who make parenting children with complex trauma their priority, there is hope. Remember that a struggling child's expressions of anger or pain are not based on an opposition toward you. Their behavior is how they've learned to protect themselves. Through the availability of a loving parent, broken trust can be slowly, methodically, and lovingly rebuilt.

Reflections

What can I do on a practical level to foster secure attachments?

Children are both a gift and responsibility. The first three years of a child's life set the stage for their sense of security. Make knowing your child's temperament, their individual cues about needs, and your response a priority.

Mindfulness, in this context, means being aware of yourself, your emotions, attitude, and behavior in relation to the developing and changing needs of your child. This is an active process of reminding yourself to be observant, in an unhurried manner, of the cues being given by your child.

Be emotionally available to your child. Put away work, put down phones, step away from the computer, and greatly limit TV time, so you can learn about your child's unique personality and cues on how to promote connection in your relationship.

Connect sensory comforts with soothing words. Gently touch and use rhythmic movement and focused eye contact. Provide food in an unhurried way—let a child "digest" and observe who you are on many nonverbal levels: smiles, animated faces, rocking, and massage.

Move with your child at a slow pace that meets the need for transitions to unfold at a manageable rate. Our society has fostered a quick pace of rushed schedules and endless obligations. Plan ahead for changes throughout the day to ensure a relaxed pace. Pack bags for tomorrow's outing tonight, think ahead in planning menus, clothes, and what is needed to make transitions easier.

When you come together before or after a period of separation (upon awakening, return from work/school, and before bed) nurture yourself and your child with lap time and intentional relaxation to promote attunement. Feel the co-regulation of shared heart rate that occurs when you enjoy this level of unhurried physical contact.

Realize that relationships are connections that can be changed by positive actions and attitude. Every day presents new opportunities.

Secure Attachment

Interactions between the Secure Parent and Child	☐ Affectionate ☐ Predictable ☐ Attuned; adept at reading cues ☐ Responsive ☐ Sensitive ☐ Safe ☐ Delight in meeting the needs of their children ☐ Are accepting of their children's distress ☐ Can discern the needs of their children without being preoccupied with their own needs ☐ Can be in control without being controlling ☐ Are not intimidated by the neediness of their children ☐ Parent can accept their own imperfections and ask for forgiveness
View of Self and Others	☐ Sees self as lovable and worthy of care ☐ Has a sense of self-efficacy and confidence ☐ Sees relationships as a source of pleasure and comfort ☐ Makes friends easily
Characteristics of Infant	☐ Molds to the body of the caregiver ☐ Calms in the presence of the primary caregiver ☐ Initiates interaction ☐ Shows a variety of emotions ☐ Curious ☐ Seeks proximity to the primary caregiver ☐ Dependent
Characteristics of Children	☐ Curious ☐ Initiates engagement with others ☐ Optimistic ☐ Trusting of others ☐ Can understand their own emotions and those of others ☐ Self reliant but balanced by ability to seek comfort from others ☐ Consistent and predictable ☐ Self-confident

Insecure Ambivalent Attachment

Interactions between the Ambivalent Parent and Child	☐ Uncertain and inconsistent; responds out of own need rather than the need of the baby (Goulding, 2014) ☐ Misattuned; inability to accurately read the baby's signals ☐ Wants to keep the child close out of own need ☐ Intrusive ☐ Child may be clingy as a way to keep the parent close
View of Self and Others	☐ Self is unworthy and incompetent ☐ Low self-efficacy ☐ Views others as unpredictable ☐ Low capacity for self-reflection
Characteristics of Infant	☐ Fretful, whiny, and clingy ☐ Hesitant to explore ☐ Displays emotion nonverbally ☐ Unable to be comforted by the attachment figure
Characteristics of Child	☐ Fears separation and not being "held in mind" ☐ Views world as black and white; parent is all good or all bad ☐ Exaggerates negative affect; resorts to theatrics Difficulty maintaining friendships—clingy and possessive ☐ Often described as attention-seeking, but is in need of attention ☐ Looks to friends for support but doesn't offer support in return ☐ Poor concentration and distractibility ☐ Will often engage in obsessive behaviors if he doesn't feel safe ☐ Prone to being victim of the bully ☐ Can be described as "in your face"

Insecure Avoidant Attachment

Characteristics of the Avoidant Parent	☐ Dismisses or devalues their child's attachment needs ☐ The neediness of their child makes them feel uncomfortable ☐ Unaffectionate ☐ Uncomfortable with touch ☐ Harsh ☐ Disengaged; distant ☐ Denies or ignores child's emotions ☐ Achievement- and task-oriented ☐ Perfectionistic ☐ Things are more important than people ☐ Uncomfortable with intimacy ☐ Lacks empathy for others
View of Self and Others	☐ Expects others to be hosti0le and rejecting ☐ Views self as unlovable and worthy
Characteristics of Infants	☐ Resists molding to the parent's body ☐ May seem withdrawn and shut down ☐ Seems not to miss caregiver; seems cool and calm ☐ More interested in things than in people ☐ Does not cry often
Characteristics of Children	☐ Very self-reliant and independent ☐ Distress is denied or minimized ☐ Refuses to accept comfort ☐ May have sudden, extreme outbursts that seem to come out of nowhere ☐ May become the bully ☐ Knows it all—to not know something makes them feel vulnerable ☐ Lack of empathy—can treat people like things ☐ Compliant ☐ Seeks to be invisible ☐ Flies under the radar to avoid harsh response ☐ Seeks to please others ☐ Cautious

Disorganized Attachment

Characteristics of the Disorganized Parent	☐ Parent is either scared or scary ☐ Behavior is unpredictable and frightening ☐ May be mentally ill ☐ Harmful by default—profound neglect ☐ May be addicted to substances ☐ Domestic violence, continuous marital strife ☐ Things are more important than people ☐ May be overwhelmed by unresolved mourning or grief ☐ Has no idea how to relate to a child ☐ Will display characteristics of both the avoidant and the ambivalent parent ☐ Detached and uninvolved
View of Self and Others	☐ Expects others to be harmful and scary ☐ Relationships are a source of fear and harm ☐ Views self as unlovable and defective
Characteristics of Infant	☐ Resists molding to the parent's body ☐ Shows fear in the presence of the caregiver; instead of being comforted, may scream ☐ Biorhythms disrupted ☐ May remain in a dissociative state
Characteristics of Children	☐ Behavior is unpredictable and random ☐ Unable to connect with another human ☐ Lives in state of chaos that is reflected in behavior ☐ Little capacity to self-reflect and be aware of an internal "self" ☐ Sense of time and a coherent life narrative is absent ☐ Lives in a heightened state of anxiety ☐ Highly vigilant and aware of distractions ☐ Lacks trust in the authority of adults ☐ Objects are more important than people ☐ Insensitive to others feelings ☐ Reactive to unseen triggers ☐ Extremely sensitive to criticism and implied humiliation ☐ Flooded by emotions which have no apparent meaning

Assess your own parent–child history, and identify the attachment style of your parents. Note specific practices, behaviors, and emotions they sent you—messages about their expectations of your behavior in response back to them.

Now look at your parenting relationship with your child. Have you transferred any of those behaviors and emotions into your own parenting style? Can you identify any of your child's behavior that might be a response to your style of parenting?

It's never too late to change patterns of behavior that aren't working. All that is required is humility, persistence, and intentional thought. Your relationships will be your reward!

Chapter Five

Connections with Toddlers:
Encouraging Safe Exploration

There is nothing more fun and fascinating than a toddler! Their newfound mobility, emerging personality, and language skills make the toddler a delightful little person to be with. The toddler years are typically defined as the period between 18 and 36 months. Despite the fact that language skills are still limited, toddlers are very adept at making their wishes, needs, and desires clearly known.

The reciprocal nature of the attachment bond becomes even stronger as the toddler is now able to actively seek proximity to Mom and Dad and initiate physical affection and interaction. Despite the increase in language, much of the communication between toddlers and their parents continues to be nonverbal. Mom and Dad's facial expressions continue to be an important component in orienting the child to his world.

The cute and cuddly infant-turned-toddler becomes a whirlwind of perpetual motion, climbing on everything, and insisting on doing things his own way. He empties the kitchen cabinets of the pots and pans, unrolls the toilet paper, and laughs while doing it. The living room furniture is his jungle gym. He throws temper tantrums when he doesn't get his way and "no, me, mine" become his favorite words. This is why many refer to the toddler years as the "terrible twos."

So what is going on here? Do these really have to be "terrible" years? Are these behaviors a mark of the toddler's rebellious nature? Is it willful defiance, or could it be something else?

The behavior of the toddler can be easily misunderstood if we do not look through the lens of child development. These years can truly be the "terrific twos" and a time of awe and wonder as Mom and Dad watch the development of their child. So how do we parent toddlers well and continue to strengthen the emotional connection?

Creating a Sense of Felt Safety

Emotional Availability

Toddlers are highly emotional little people and sometimes experience strong feelings that can overwhelm them. The manner in which Mom or Dad responds to their emotions is important. When parents respond to, and don't avoid, the intense anger and frustration of a toddler with a calming and supportive presence, it reassures the toddler that Mom and Dad are psychologically big enough to take care of him.

The toddler comes to realize, "The world isn't going to fall apart when I do. Mom and Dad aren't going to come undone when I do. Mom and Dad are big enough to keep me safe."

If a parent reacts to a toddler's temper tantrum with anger, frustration, or withdrawal, the child experiences fear and anxiety. *If Mom and Dad can't handle my big emotions, then how can I?*

This is why predictability is so crucial for your child—even when it's difficult for you, and *especially* when it's difficult for you.

Predictability

The brain hates chaos and unpredictability. By the time the child reaches toddlerhood, his biological rhythms with regard to eating, sleeping, waking, and playing have assimilated into the schedule of the family. Creating a sense of routine and "sameness" helps the toddler feel safe.

Establishing routines can make life run more smoothly for the entire family. This allows both parents and children to invest their emotional energies in connecting. The morning routine is extremely important, especially if both parents are working and the toddler is in childcare. How families begin the day sets the emotional tone for the entire day. Some things to think about:

- How do I awaken my toddler? Do I stand in the kitchen and shout? Or yell from the bottom of the stairs? Do they awaken on their own? If so, how do I respond to them when they come pitter patting into my room and wake me up?

- Do I make time to cuddle, read, or simply hold my toddler for a few minutes? Or am I in a chaotic rush to get out the door?

- How do I decide what my toddler is going to wear? Do I give her two choices the night before and have it laid out? Or, do I tell my child what she is going to wear as we are getting dressed? Am I scrambling around the house looking for clean clothes, thereby stressing myself out as well as my child?

- How and when do we eat breakfast? Do we eat before we get dressed? After we get dressed? How do we decide what to eat? Do I have a routine menu? Do I grab the first thing I see in the cabinet? Do I give my toddler a choice between two things, or do I decide for him?

- What is the bedtime routine? Do we eat snack or read a story before or after we take a bath? Do I lie beside them or expect them to go to sleep on their own? Do both Mom and Dad play a part in bedtime routines with each child, or do we "divide and conquer?"

I (Barbara) struggled with "sameness" and predictability when my children were young. Because of my husband's quadriplegia, medical emergencies happened on a regular basis. Our youngest daughter also experienced serious medical issues at age two. There were many disruptions to our daily routine that were beyond my control. I strived to keep our morning and bedtime routines the same. If we could at least begin and end the day with a sense of predictability, it made our lives easier—and my children had at least some sense of normalcy.

It's also important to realize that predictability isn't necessarily about clock time. We got up and went to bed approximately at the same time, but we weren't militant about the clock. If a neighbor came by and bedtime was delayed twenty minutes, it was all good. Predictability was more about doing the same things in the same order, day in and day out.

I recently explained this to a dad who was recently discharged from the military. We were talking about clock time vs. predictability of events. His face immediately brightened and he said, "Oh, I get it. In the military, we call it event planning. We may not know the time a particular event takes place, but we always know the order in which it plays out." Event planning helps all children feel safe.

Touch

Touch continues to be an important form of connection with toddlers. Their increasing mobility enables them to initiate and seek out contact and playful touch. They crawl into Mom and Dad's lap, wrap themselves around your leg, crawl in bed with you, pinch your nose, tickle your chin, and throw their arms around you in a bear hug.

Responding with warmth and affection is natural for most parents. There is nothing that makes my heart happy like getting a hug from my two-year-old grandson. There is just something about the unbridled affection of a toddler that brings joy to the soul and hope to keep on keeping on—no matter how hard life can be. It's the ultimate reward for all the inconveniences parenting sometimes brings.

If you find yourself uncomfortable with giving or receiving touch from your child, it's important to look at your own childhood and think about the messages that were communicated to you about touch. Some families are very touchy-feely, and others rarely touch at all.

A friend related that she had no memories of being hugged or touched as a child by either one of her parents. When she had her first baby, she found herself weeping one day as she sat and rocked her newborn. At first she thought she was crazy, but she found herself thinking over and over, *How could a mom not hug her child?* She found that unfathomable.

This was the first time it occurred to her that she had no memories of being touched by her parents. She reported that over the years as

74

she rocked, hugged, and cuddled with her children, she found healing and discovered the joy and pleasure of physical closeness.

As time went on, she learned more about the history of her parents—the hardships and challenges they faced in their own childhood. The more she learned about her own family history, the more it made sense that touch was not part of the dynamic of her family of origin. But, as often happens, this wound that she felt earlier slowly began to heal as she gave her children what she never had.

In giving, she found healing. You can, too. Healing can also be found in playfulness.

Simple childhood games such as Pat-a-Cake, This Little Piggy, and Peek-a-Boo not only provide playful touch, but also build important cognitive skills. Piggyback rides, blowing raspberries on tummies, and riding on a parent's shoulders are fun ways of physically connecting. Toddlers beckon parents to chase them. They flop into your lap while you read, and they invite you to roughhouse.

Infant massage continues to be valuable as the child moves in toddler stage. And the massage strokes used on smaller children can be adapted for a physically larger child. By the time a child reaches toddlerhood, massage may become a regular and routine part of the day.

Toddlers love to sit with Mom and Dad to read books. Rocking, cuddling, and snuggling together build strong connections. Making meaningful touch a part of your daily routine is important to a child's development.

Tone of Voice

Our tone of voice is another important way of creating a sense of felt safety, just as it did in infancy. Many of us continue to use the language of "mother-ese" with our toddlers.

However, with their growing sense of autonomy, toddlers increasingly engage in activities and behaviors that require the imposition of limits and elicit a stern "no" from Mom and Dad. Toddlers dump out the trash can, unroll the toilet paper, and empty the cabinets at the most inconvenient times. At the end of the day, parents are often exhausted from trying to meet the demands of parenthood and work. They can find themselves speaking in a harsh tone of voice that can sound loud and demanding.

It's always okay to be firm but never okay to be harsh. We send powerful messages to children simply through our tone. Our tone of voice is interpreted and perceived at a very unconscious level and either creates a sense of safety or fear.

When I want to set firm limits and communicate a sense that "I mean business" without frightening the child, I find it helpful to think in terms of lowering the tone of my voice and slowing my words down. It's not scary, and it's not harsh. And it sends a very clear message to the child's brain: I mean what I say.

If we speak to toddlers in a harsh tone of voice on a consistent basis, they will live in a persistent state of fear. Fear creates disconnection.

Eye Contact

As toddlers grow in their autonomy and test the limits of their own power and the boundaries that are set for them, our feelings may fluctuate throughout the day. Fortunately, their cuteness factor can offset the irritation that can arise when they climb on the kitchen counter for the tenth time. But sometimes, in moments of high stress or fatigue, our feelings spill over. We might not verbalize anything, but our face says it all.

Our eyes are particularly reflective of how we feel. Soft eyes communicate love and acceptance. Bright, shining eyes portray joy. A hard, steely glare communicates anger and rejection. The eyes never lie. Toddlers are always watching and attuning to the face of Mom and Dad to determine what is acceptable and what is not. The watchfulness of toddlers plays a huge role in the development of conscience.

The child pulls the cat's tail and immediately checks Mom's facial expression or Dad's reaction. They pick up the potted plant and prepare to throw it. Dad leaps from his chair to retrieve it with a look of "Oh no, don't you dare." The toddler receives the message loud and clear that his behavior is not okay.

Creating a Toddler-Friendly Home

Notice that the title of this section isn't, "Creating a Toddler Dominated Home." There is a vast difference between a home that is child friendly and one that is dominated by a child of any age.

Children are born with a God-given desire to explore and master their world. They come packaged with an enormous curiosity to figure out how things work. This is how they learn. This is how they grow.

The inquisitiveness of a toddler and his propensity to "get into everything" is not a sign of rebellion or "naughty" behavior. It is a mark of God's design.

This is important to grasp because if I view the inquisitiveness of the toddler and his propensity to make messes as evidence of his disobedience then I am likely to respond in a punitive manner. This will not only squelch his curiosity, but also undermine the emotional connection that I am striving to develop. The Scriptures say, "Train up a child in the way he should go, and when he is old, he will not depart from it." If we look at the original text, this verse says, "Train up a child in the way he is bent." Honoring what we know about child development is considering the "bent" of the child.

So the challenge is to balance the toddler's need to explore with the need to keep him safe—and to maintain our sanity. Of course I don't want my child to unroll the toilet paper every day, so I keep the bathroom door shut. I put the Tupperware and pots and pans in the lower cabinets and put the glass bakeware up high. I leave the inexpensive and unbreakable trinkets out on the coffee table but put the family heirlooms out of reach. I don't want him climbing on the furniture and kitchen counters, so I give him something appropriate to climb on. I might buy a Little Tykes slide or put a stack of bed pillows on the floor for him to climb on.

The goal is always to accommodate the developmental need of the toddler without compromising safety and reason. The following scenario took place in the home of someone we know, and illustrates the effects of not understanding a toddler's intention.

Two-year-old Jason was fascinated by the beautiful ornaments on the Christmas tree. He stood in front of the tree gazing at the lights, completely enraptured with its spectacle. He approached the tree, stuck out his finger, and gingerly touched a lovely-but-breakable Christmas ornament. Dad was standing nearby and observed his son's behavior. When he saw the child move toward the tree, he lurched into action, got down on one knee, angrily peered into the child's face, pointed his finger and shouted, "Don't you dare touch that tree. You touch that tree again and you will get a spanking."

A look of terror came across Jason's face, and he recoiled from his father. For a brief moment, it was as if he was frozen in time. When he recovered, he began to cry, frantically looked about for his mother, and ran to her.

So let's think about what just happened. It is clear that the father assumes his son's behavior is willful disobedience. *He is touching the Christmas ornament because he chooses to disobey.* The father responds in a punitive and shaming manner. The child is left in a state of fear and moves away from the father, seeking comfort from Mom. Dad walks away from this scenario with a ruptured emotional connection between himself and his child.

Let's consider another scenario in a home that is child friendly.

Two-year-old Jason was fascinated by the beautiful ornaments on the Christmas tree. He approached the tree, stuck out his finger, and gingerly touched a lovely-but-breakable Christmas ornament. Dad was standing nearby and observed his son's behavior. When he saw the child move toward the tree, he bent down and said, "They sure are pretty. You like those sparkling red ornaments. But you know what? They can easily break, and the broken glass would hurt you. Let's move this ornament to the top of the tree, and let's put some other non-breakable things down here."

Dad removed a few plastic ornaments from the top and allowed Jason to hang them on the bottom of the tree. Dad put his arm around Jason and they observed the beautiful tree together. Jason's need to explore and touch is met; he is kept safe; and the beauty of the family Christmas tree is preserved. Dad and Jason walk away with their emotional connection strengthened.

Attunement to the Emotional Life of Toddlers

If we're going to form an enduring emotional bond between ourselves and our toddler, it is important that we understand the emotional life of toddlers and what makes them tick. Knowing what's happening within the child allows us "see, hear, and understand" them. Let's begin with a toddler's seemingly favorite word.

A Declaration of Independence

Why do toddlers love the word, "no"?

In the first year of life, there are very few reasons to say "no" to an infant. During infancy, a child's emotional bucket is filled with hundreds and thousands of yes answers. When a baby cries and I feed him in a timely and sensitive manner, I say, yes to the child's needs and I put a yes in his bucket.

When a child cries in discomfort from a soiled diaper and I change the diaper in a timely and sensitive manner, I add another yes to his bucket. The child emerges at the end of the first year with a bucket full of yes answers that contribute to his knowing he is worthy of love and care. He knows his needs are a priority in the family by the consistency and timeliness of the response.

But this quickly changes in toddlerhood. As the child becomes more mobile, the likelihood of "getting into trouble" with Mom and Dad increases and he begins to accumulate a bucket of no answers.

Also at eighteen months, children begin to realize they are a separate individual with their own opinions, preferences, emotions, thoughts, and desires. They're becoming aware of their own *inner* life. As awareness of their individuality grows, they experiment with this newly discovered realization and "practice" asserting their independence.

The no of a toddler, therefore, is usually a declaration of independence and not the no of rebellion. This is important to understand because if I take it personally and interpret their no as evidence of their rebellious nature, then I am likely to respond with power and control. And likely to be embroiled with my toddler on a daily basis.

I have to find a way to balance their need for independence with their need for structure. That's a tall order for parents. I have a friend who says during this stage of development, parents need to be the "benevolent dictator."

So how do we serve as the "benevolent dictator?" Don't take the no of a toddler personally. Don't engage and try to rationalize with him—you are spitting in the wind. Ignore the no, and give him two choices.

Barbara gives an example: *One evening when my granddaughter was two, I walked into the living room just as her dad told her it was time to go to bed. In classic two-year-old form she replied, "No. I not tired."*

My son-in-law looked at me and said, "She's yours."

I ignored the no and gave her two yeses by saying, "Would you like a piggy back ride or would you like to walk like a gorilla?"

She immediately responded, "I want a gorilla piggy back ride." She climbed on my back and off to bed we went with no protest.

So what happened here? Ignoring the no and giving two yeses assumes obedience. Going to bed is nonnegotiable; how she gets there is. She can have a piggy back ride or walk like a gorilla, but one way or the other, she is going to bed. In this interaction, I honored her need to assert herself and that's have some control. But at the same time, I communicated an expectation of obedience.

I was in control without being controlling.

Being in control without being controlling is a critical understanding for parents at all stages of development. I always need to be the "boss", but I can do that without being "bossy." What would this scenario have looked like if I responded in a controlling manner? Let's think about it.

"No. I not tired."

I think to myself, I'm going to nip this rebellion in the bud, and respond by saying, "You need to march yourself right up to bed immediately. Do as you are told."

She throws herself on the floor and starts screaming. I pick her up and take her upstairs while she protests, "I don't want to. I'm not tired." I basically have to wrestle with her to get her pajamas on. Her cries get louder and more intense. Soon she is beside herself in a complete emotional meltdown. I have made my point—she is going to bed whether she wants to or not. But she is in a state of emotional disintegration. I have forced compliance and ruptured the connection. I have gained nothing.

Saying No to a Toddler

What do you do when no is the only option? For example, getting buckled into a car seat is nonnegotiable. Inevitably there comes a time when you must go home after a birthday party or an outing at the park. It's always helpful to give toddlers a warning that it is almost time leave. Demanding that they abruptly stop playing and leave is almost certain to evoke some pushback. Even adults like to bring closure to an activity before transitioning to another. Whenever possible, alerting your toddler that you will be leaving soon allows him to know what is coming next instead of being a complete surprise.

Predictability brings a sense of safety.

It is highly likely that, despite your advance warning, you will still get some pushback. Acknowledging your child's desires before kindly but firmly saying no can help buffer some of the distress. *For example, I invited a young, single mom and her two-year-old daughter to the house for lunch. We played dolls, picked flowers, and went for a walk. When it came time to go home, she feigned sleepiness and lay on my couch, pretending to snore. Mom told her she could have five more minutes to play and then they would leave.*

As soon as Mom said this, the child popped up and went back to playing. After a period of time, Mom once again told the child it was time to leave. She suddenly became very sleepy again and lay down on the couch, pretending to sleep. Mom once again gave her five more minutes to play.

I knew where this was going, so I went over and said, "We have had such a good time today, and I know it is hard to stop playing when you're having fun. But it is time to go home. Let's put the babies to bed." We wrapped up the dolls and put them on the couch to "sleep." Then I took her by the hand and said, "It's time to go to the car."

She balked and said, "No, Miss Barbara."

I picked her up and said, "It is so hard to stop playing when you are having a good time. We played dolls, picked flowers, and took a walk. We had such a good time. But it is time to go home."

As we walked to the car she said over and over, "No, Miss Barbara."

And I kept saying over and over, "I know it is hard to stop playing, but it is time to go home." I buckled her into her seat. Despite her protests, she compliantly allowed me to buckle her into her seat.

I acknowledged her desire to continue playing before saying no. By picking her up when she resisted going to the car, I communicated to her that I was "big enough" to take care of her. By gently but firmly placing her in the car seat, I communicated that I meant business. This interaction was not harsh or shaming.

By the way, getting buckled into a car seat is often stressful for toddlers. There are many reasons for this. Toddlerhood is a time of exploration and discovery. By nature, toddlers are very active. Riding in a car seat requires a toddler to override their natural tendencies. It also involves a great deal of stimulation to the sensory processing system which, in and of itself, can be stressful. When you consider all of these factors, it is easy to understand why getting buckled in can be so hard.

Here are some strategies that may help.

1. Begin telling your child a story as you prepare to go to the car. Build up to a suspenseful ending, and tell your child you will finish the story when he gets buckled in his seat.

2. Give your child a choice as to how he moves to the car: jumping, tiptoeing, stomping, etc.

3. Give your toddler some "deep muscle input." Let them hold something to squeeze.

4. Give your child a snack to eat.

5. Listen to familiar songs. Melodic melodies and rhythm stimulate the safety center of the brain and can help calm your child.

Why Do Toddlers Love the Words, "Me" and "Mine"?

As toddlers become aware of their own preferences, wants, and wishes, they become possessive of their things, and "me" and "mine" become their new favorite words. Another child reaches for their toy, and the toddler starts pushing and screaming, "mine!"

Their inability to share and take turns is the result of a developmental incapacity to take the perspective of another. They are not able to "walk in someone else's shoes" so to speak.

When a toddler walks up to another child and grabs a toy, eliciting a blood-curdling scream, it is a surprise to the toddler. It never occurs to them that someone else also wants the toy. *I want the toy and everyone knows that*—or so they think.

So the challenge then becomes for parents to attune to the developmental capacities of the toddler while at the same time gently nudging the child into new understandings. Fortunately when it comes to sharing possessions and turn-taking, toddlers are easily distracted.

When your toddler grabs a toy out of the hands of another, you simply give it back to the other child and say something like, "No, that's his. Let's find something for you to play with." You immediately direct the child's attention to something that you know they enjoy. You might roll a beach ball to him. Or you can pick the child up and move the child to a different location and engage his attention in looking out the window, looking at a book, or talking to another adult.

Distraction is a strategy that toddlers respond to much of the time. The key is finding something else that engages their attention, and the previously desired object is quickly forgotten.

We know what you're thinking. *But what if my toddler has a meltdown and goes ballistic?*

That is likely to happen now and then. First, I acknowledge my toddler's desire. "I know you love to play with that toy." Then, I use some kind of rhythmic touch or rhythmic movement to calm the child. I might pick him up, bounce, rock, or sway gently and talk soothingly. "I know you love playing with the toy he has. When you're ready, we will find a different toy."

Attuning to your toddler means recognizing their developmental incapacities to share and take turns. It means not expecting them to do something they are incapable of doing.

Why Are Toddlers Prone to Meltdowns?

There are many factors that contribute to temper tantrums, but the most common causes are fatigue, hunger, and overstimulation. When you are out in public and see children go into meltdown mode, look at your watch. It's often around mealtime. When blood sugar starts to drop, behavior also deteriorates. When fatigue sets in, even the best of us have trouble behaving well.

Every child has a threshold of too much stimulation. Getting in and out of the car a half-dozen times in a morning and visiting multiple stores can be taxing. Attuned parents are aware of their toddlers' hunger patterns and signals that they are done.

We've all been there—we have a long list of errands that have to get done before that vacation or before the relatives arrive. We get halfway through our agenda, and our toddler loses it. The constant in and out of the car, in and out of a shopping cart, the hustle and bustle take its toll, and we have a screaming toddler on our hands. In these moments, what they need most is to be held, rocked, and soothed.

These kinds of scenes are inevitable and understandable when they happen now and then. But when we consistently ignore our toddler's basic patterns of functioning and overstimulate them on a regular basis, we undermine the emotional connection.

Creating a Play-Based Environment

One of the joys of parenting a toddler is their playfulness. Toddlers initiate many playful experiences that are actually attachment rituals.

They invite Mom and Dad to play chase by looking over their shoulder, giggling and running in the opposite direction. Can you imagine how a toddler would feel if they looked over their shoulder only to see Mom looking at her cell phone instead of chasing? It would not take too many moments of nonengagement before the toddler would give up and never initiate.

Toddlers love hide and seek, Ring around the Rosie, and piggy back rides. They like to "volley" with Mom and Dad by throwing a ball, playing Pat-a-Cake, or Peek-a-Boo. Many start to enjoy rough-and-tumble play with parents and older brothers and sisters.

They may invite you to read with them by plopping a book in your lap. Rocking, cuddling, and snuggling while reading together has profound emotional—as well as cognitive—benefit. The child comes to associate reading with joy and pleasure.

Responding to a toddler's initiations to play is as important as feeding them. Following their lead and accepting their invitation to play in a certain way or with a particular toy is a powerful way a parent demonstrates respect for the child's interests—and reinforces a child's sense of self-efficacy. Playful engagement fills the child's tank with feelings of joy and connection.

If we only play the role of policemen and never the role of playmate, strong emotional connections will be undermined. When we follow children's lead in play, they are more likely to cooperate with us in those moments when compliance is needed. When we hijack children's play and try to divert their attention something we enjoy more, we undermine strong emotional connections.

I (Cathy) was recently observing the interaction between a mom and a toddler. *The toddler rolled a beach ball to Mom and eagerly waited for her to return the ball. Mom pushed the ball aside and beckoned the child to sit by her and do a puzzle. The toddler ran to get the ball and threw it toward her. Once again, she ignored his initiation and beckoned him to come sit beside her. He ran off to the other side of the room to play with something else.*

Reflections

Watching a toddler explore and discover newfound abilities is perhaps one of the most delightful stages of child development. The enthusiasm of a toddler is contagious and invites you to join in the fun that few can refuse. Coupled with the delight, the toddler begins to learn how to express and exert preferences with boundless energy.

Application

Many of the strategies mentioned in this chapter apply to children of all ages. This week try a couple of them.

1. Ignore their no and give two yeses from which to choose with enthusiasm.

2. At a moment of impasse, acknowledge your child's intent or desire before you say no.

3. Before transitioning to another activity or location, give your child a warning to allow for closure.

4. Follow the lead of the child in play. Engage in an activity that he clearly enjoys and initiates.

5. Engage in rough-and-tumble play, if your child clearly indicates that they enjoy it.

6. Read to your child.

Chapter Six

Temperamental Differences:
Attuning to Your Child's Temperament

The essence of attunement throughout childhood is to communicate to our children, *"I see you. I hear you. I understand you."* We see and hear our children through much more than our eyes and ears. We observe with all of our senses so we can understand and connect to the heart of our child.

Truly "seeing" our children means we notice: we notice what makes them happy, what makes them scared, what makes them sad, and what makes them angry. We know that they prefer to have their backs rubbed at night rather than patted. We know that they love to play "tickle monster" with Dad and read books with Mom.

We also see and notice their temperamental differences. By the time children reach toddlerhood, their temperamental differences are clearly discernible. A simple definition of temperament refers to the mental, physical, and emotional characteristics that remain consistent over time. A child's temperament is fundamentally about how they approach the world. Some approach life with great gusto and enthusiasm while others are more timid and reticent. Recognizing our child's temperament can help us forge strong emotional connections.

Identification of Children's Temperaments

Temperament refers to a child's typical way of thinking, behaving or reacting in the day-to-day world. Most experts believe that there is a biological basis to temperament that is part of the genetic makeup. In assessing the temperamental bent of a child, there are nine basic characteristics that are considered:

1. Activity Level. Some children are very laid back and are content just observing the action. They prefer calm and quiet activities. Other children are active from the start. Even as infants, they wiggle and squirm, twist and turn. When they reach the toddler years, they are always on the move, running, climbing, and scurrying about.

2. Adaptability. Some children find it very challenging to move from one setting to another or from one activity to another. They tend to be rigid and don't handle transitions well. Others are very adaptable to the ups and downs and changes in life. They can fall asleep in the stroller at the mall just as well as they can sleep in their bed at home.

3. Approachability. Some children are cautious about meeting new people and approaching new situations. When they meet someone new, they want and need plenty of time to "warm up" to the individual. On the other hand, there are other toddlers who never meet a stranger. They immediately warm up to people and embrace them as if they were best friends.

4. Distractibility. Some children seem almost oblivious to what is going on around them and are not easily pulled away from what they are doing. Others notice everything and get easily sidetracked from one thing to another.

5. Intensity. Some children are more subdued in their emotional expressions and reactions and appear calm and mellow. Sometimes it is difficult to discern what they are feeling at all. Others respond in a big way with *big* emotions. They have a meltdown when they are upset and squeal with delight when they are happy.

6. Persistence. Some children give up very easily, and others have dogged determination despite obstacles. The persistent child only gives

up reluctantly, whereas the reluctant child lacks the drive to self-motivate to the finish line.

7. Positivity or mood. Some children are more melancholy and approach life with a very serious tone. They struggle with having a positive attitude and don't laugh or smile easily. Others have a sunny disposition and never seem to be bothered by much of anything. They laugh easily and often.

8. Regularity. Some children's biorhythms are unpredictable and chaotic. There is no pattern to their sleeping, eating, and elimination habits. Others eat, sleep, and have bowel movements on a very predictable schedule.

9. Sensitivity. Some children are unfazed by changes in light, temperature, noises, tastes, and textures. Others are highly sensitive to and detect even subtle differences in the environment and react to them. They can be picky eaters and highly aware of the texture of their clothes.

Categories of Temperament

Based on these nine characteristics, child development experts have identified four broad categories of temperament:

1. The "Easygoing" child. This child is one who adapts easily to new situations and people. They are not easily upset or distracted. They are fairly predictable in their functioning and don't present serious behavioral challenges.

2. The "Slow to warm up" child. This child is one who takes some time to adjust to new situations and people by standing back and observing. But once they do, they are "all-in."

3. The "Difficult" child. This child is very unpredictable, and their biorhythms are irregular. They can be hard to please and have intense reactions to life.

4. The "Active" child. This child is one who is perpetually on the go and is often described as into everything. They have high levels of

curiosity, which makes them unafraid of trying new things to the point of sometimes venturing into more risky behaviors.

Identifying basic temperamental tendencies enables parents to more easily look at life through the eyes of their child.

For example, if I have a two-year-old daughter who is slow to warm up, I will need to take this into consideration when I enroll her in a mother's day out program. Before spending all day in the program, I might visit the classroom and meet the teacher at a time when other children are not there. I might go back another day with other children present and let her spend some time observing. She could then go back a third day, and if she appears comfortable, she would remain for the day. If she is still anxious, I might pick her up after a few hours and increase the length of her stay over time.

The Match of Parent–Child Temperaments

Problems can arise when the parent and child have opposite temperaments. For example, if Dad is a very active, outgoing person who loves extreme sports, he might have difficulty relating to his "fearful" child who prefers more sedentary and "artsy" activities. Dad might get frustrated when he takes his child to the company Christmas party and the child quietly sits in the corner while Dad is the life of the party.

Having opposite personalities does not always mean problems. But it does mean that the burden of attunement lies with the parent being willing to "cross the street", so to speak, and look at the world through the eyes of the child and make adjustments accordingly.

Another difficult match can be when a parent and a child have similar personalities. For example, Mom is a very high-needs "difficult" personality and so is the child. Conflicting needs may be a challenge to navigate when both are very demanding and find it difficult to compromise.

Attunement as a Two-Way Street

Self-awareness—or mindfulness, as it is sometimes called—is critical for parents. I need to be aware of when my patience is pushed to the limit, or if I'm exhausted and my frustration level is high.

The truth is, we all "leak." Our feelings toward others have a tendency to leak out no matter how hard we try to conceal them. This is especially true for those with whom we live. In moments such as

90

these, we need to take some time to regroup before we deal with the challenges at hand.

This is the benefit of two-parent families. When one parent has reached their limit, ideally, the other one can step in and provide relief. This is also the challenge of single-parent homes. There is no one to help buffer the stress. Having a supportive network of friends and a faith community can be enormously helpful.

Accepting my Child For Who He Is

An enormous amount of time and energy in our culture are focused on getting children "ready" for the next phase of development. When I fail to see my child for who he is right now—not what I want him to be next year—I place inappropriate expectations upon him that results in a discouraged child.

When I'm constantly focused on the person I want my child to become, I'm unable to see and love him for the child he is today. Attunement is undermined, and connections are weakened.

When we give our children what they need today, they will automatically be ready for tomorrow. The developmental needs of a three-year-old are very different than those of a four-year-old. We do our children no favors when we expect them to function at a different level.

Reflections

Spend some time reflecting on the characteristics of your own temperament. Which broad category would you fall into? What are the practical implications of your temperament for new experiences, situations that elicit feelings of fear, or challenging tasks requiring motivation and completion?

Now, look at the same in regard to your child. What approach do you take to provide the necessary support for your child given their temperament?

Do you help your easily frustrated child to identify small steps to a desired goal? Do you encourage him along the way as he stays the course with perseverance? Do you provide gentleness to the child who is slow to warm up, allowing them the time to find their comfort zone?

No human being falls into one temperament category; we're all a unique mix. Utilize an understanding of temperaments to help attune to your child, but do not label them.

Practice mindfulness in situations requiring transitions, both large and small, and help your child develop confidence based on their temperament. Proactively think through the new situations with which your child is confronted: new classes every year in school, preparing for the music recital, stopping an activity to prepare for bedtime, saying goodbye to a friend, or leaving the birthday party. When we establish routines and rituals to help our child develop self-understanding and successfully manage their own approaches to daily life, we enable them to trust in their internal tendencies—and their God-given design.

Chapter Seven

Promoting Attachment with Your Preschooler: Tell Me Why

The preschool years are typically defined as the period between 36 and 60 months. This is a fun and exciting time for both parents and children. The child's personality and temperament are clearly evident, and they approach the world with a great deal of exuberance and enthusiasm. They are enormously inquisitive, and their curiosity knows no bounds.

Their new favorite word is *Why*. They are far more independent in taking care of many of their basic needs such as eating and toileting, yet their need for strong emotional connections remains a priority. Independence does not mean weakening or severing the emotional connection.

Felt Safety

As children move into the preschool years, the attachment relationship increasingly shifts from a primary drive for physical closeness to a drive for emotional closeness. Preschool children are no longer dependent upon their attachment figures to feed and dress them. They are increasingly aware of what is safe and what is not safe and capable of entertaining themselves for short periods of time with minimal supervision. When development is progressing on a positive trajectory, preschoolers move from a closeness based on physical proximity to an emotional closeness that will continue to be forged over a lifetime.

The drive for emotional connection increases while the drive for physical proximity decreases.

This is not to say that physical safety isn't a concern. Preschoolers are still exploring the limits of their capabilities and figuring out what is safe and what is not. The emotional safety of the preschool child is becoming a greater concern as parents seek to protect them from societal forces, experiences, and people that may undermine the physical, emotional, mental, and spiritual health of the child.

Creating a sense of emotional safety for our children is sometimes more elusive and less obvious than accommodating their physical safety. Emotional safety is as much about who we are as it is about what we do. Our tone of voice, demeanor and body language are just as important as our words.

Eye Contact

By the time a child is four, they have mastered the English language, and they are very proud of their accomplishment. The incessant chatter of a preschooler can be taxing to even the most patient parent. The constant, "Why?" can begin to sound like a broken record.

In moments when we have answered our child's question for the 49th time in a single day, it is easy to absentmindedly answer our children without stopping to look at them much less make eye contact. As I'm writing this, it suddenly occurs to me that maybe one of the reasons they ask the same thing over and over is because what they are really wanting is our full presence and intentional eye contact. The actual question is just a way to connect.

Eye contact is an unspoken invitation to connect. It communicates to the child that he is important and you value what he has to say. It indicates you are fully present, a gift that is increasingly rare in a distracted culture. Looking a child in the eye communicates he is a priority.

Tone of Voice

Though we no longer speak to our preschoolers in "motherese," our tone of voice continues to be a major factor in communicating a sense of felt safety. Yelling at our children in moments of anger can undermine connection—but using a tone of disgust or loathing is even worse.

I attended a conference where Dr. Vincent Feletti, primary investigator of the Adverse Childhood Experiences Study, was speaking. His research focused on the toxic effects of early adversity, which would include physical and emotional abuse, physical and emotional neglect, sexual abuse, living with someone who is mentally ill or abusing substances, and divorce or abandonment. When Dr. Felitti was asked if any of the previously mentioned adverse experiences were more toxic than the others, his answer surprised me.

He said humiliation had a slight edge over all other forms of abuse.

We live in a culture where humiliation of children is an accepted form of "discipline." We communicate a sense of humiliation to our children through our tone of voice as well as our words. *How* I say something is just as important as *what* I say. I can say to my child, "Way to go, son!" in a way that is encouraging or in a way that humiliates, depending upon my tone.

Speaking to my child in a "safe" tone doesn't mean that I'm always using a playful and light tone of voice. In moments where correction and instruction are needed, I communicate through my tone of voice that I mean business. I don't do this by yelling and screaming. I do this by slowing my cadence and lowering my tone. I can be firm without being harsh. I can communicate to my child, "I'm serious," without being scary.

Touch

Though preschool children are fully mobile and don't require the intensity of touch that an infant needs, they still seek physical closeness and affection. Touch is still a powerful tool in building and maintaining strong emotional connections. After I visited my four-year-old granddaughter, she reported to her mom, "When Nana hugs me, I feel like the most important person in the world."

Bear hugs, holding hands at the mall, riding on Dad's shoulders, "horseback" rides, tickling, and rough-and-tumble play are affectionate forms of touch that can strengthen connections.

A word of caution when dealing with a child who has a "fearful" or timid temperament: Not all children enjoy boisterous physical play. I have seen parents playfully turn their children upside down or spin them around, ignoring their protests to stop. It is likely that these children have some issues with sensory processing, and their discomfort with this form of play is very real and very frightening. Respecting our child's limits and requests to stop models respect for

97

another person's boundaries and will only increase the likelihood that they will honor other people's boundaries—including ours.

Through touch, tone of voice, and eye contact, we send powerful messages that we are a safe person that our preschooler can trust. But to further understand how to create a sense of felt safety, it is important to know the four core fears of children.

Alicia Lieberman (2009) identifies four core fears that lay at the heart of every child:

1. Fear of abandonment. A young child has an innate sense of his vulnerability and inability to take care of himself. Death of a parent is obviously a devastating blow, but there are other situations that can threaten a child with a sense of abandonment. Divorce, deployment, incarceration, and frequent absence due to work schedules can cause a child to experience a sense of abandonment.

The choices that we make as parents with regard to careers and marriage need to be informed choices made with the best interest of our children in mind. When we choose to bring a child into the world, it is no longer about "me" but about "us."

This does not mean that the decision to be in the military is wrong or to be avoided. But it does mean that I need to be intentional about maintaining connections with my child and mindful of their fear of abandonment. In situations where separation is unavoidable, there are steps a parent can take to reassure the child of their love and concern. Using video technologies that allow for face-to-face communication can reassure the child that your absence doesn't mean you have abandoned them.

The absent parent can communicate to a child that you "hold them in mind" in small but meaningful ways. You may know that your preschooler loves rocks. While away on a tour of duty or traveling with your job, you find an interesting rock that you bring home, or mail as a surprise. You might read a bedtime story over the phone or mail a card with a loving note and a sticker. These small gestures of affection or indications that "I hold you close even when I am away" can maintain a sense of emotional connection.

Understanding a child's primal fear of abandonment also means that we cannot prey upon this fear to manipulate the behavior of our child. When my preschooler refuses to get out of the car, I can't threaten to leave him in there and go into the store. If my child refuses to leave the park, I can't threaten to leave without him. I pick him up and carry him home or to the car.

The fear of abandonment also has implications for how we say goodbye to our preschooler when we drop him off at preschool or childcare. It is important to leave our child with the memory of an affectionate goodbye. It is never okay to sneak out or leave our child without letting him know we are making an exit out of a desire to avoid protest and crying.

When we leave our children without saying goodbye, we teach them that people disappear without warning. This only makes them more anxious and hypervigilant because unpredictability causes children to live in a state of fear.

2. Fear of physical harm. Our brains are wired for survival. Anytime our brain perceives someone or something that poses a potential threat, our brain triggers a "fight, flight, or freeze" reaction. This is why physical punishment, humiliation, or other fearful actions or reactions of parents cause children to physically and emotionally recoil from us. (We'll discuss corporal punishment in a later chapter.) To create a sense of felt safety, parents cannot be physically or emotionally threatening.

3. Fear of being viewed as a bad child. At the heart of every child, even the most rebellious teenager, is a desire for Mom and Dad to believe in and recognize their "goodness." They long to receive our unconditional positive regard, even when they are most unlovely. When their behavior is most unlovable, our children need us to believe in their goodness the most. To be seen as a "bad" child undermines secure attachment relationships.

Preschoolers begin to wrestle with existential issues such as love and hate, good and evil, power and vulnerability, life and death, weakness and strength, purpose and meaning, and issues of spirituality. To be viewed as a "bad" boy or girl is terrifying to a child—and undermines a child's fundamental belief that they are lovable and worthy of love and care. This has enormous implications for how we discipline not only our preschoolers but our children throughout childhood.

4. Fear of losing love. All children, at the core of their being, long for and desire the love and affection of Mom and Dad. Because our preschoolers are still figuring out what is "good" and what is "bad,"

and are still learning how to "be" in the world, parents must be willing to embrace and love their preschoolers in the midst of their "undoneness."

Years ago, I had a sign that said, "Please be patient. God is not finished with me yet." This sign is certainly appropriate when we think about our preschoolers. They are still figuring it all out. They are going to have moments of meltdown, pushback, and noncompliance. These are the moments when we need to bring them close instead of pushing them away. These are the moments when they need our love and loving guidance the most. These are the moments where we can potentially strengthen the growth of healthy attachment.

Media Exposure

Years ago, I had a three-year-old child in my preschool program who was one of the most fearful and insecure children I've ever met. She cried every day when Mom left. She stood by my side most of the day and would rarely venture out to play with other children. Attempts to encourage her to go down the slide or engage in dramatic play with other children were generally refused. She would only play with me or with another adult.

This little girl was an only child, and Mom quit her job to stay home with her. Mom was clearly resentful that she had "sacrificed so much" and yet this child was extremely insecure. As I developed a relationship with Mom, it become clear that a huge part of the problem was the fact that this child was exposed to media and life circumstances that were inappropriate for a child her age.

For her fourth birthday, she received her own personal copy of the video, *Dirty Dancing*. At preschool, she would talk about TV shows that contained adult content inappropriate for a preschooler. When her grandfather was in the hospital dying, she was taken to see him. For days, she anxiously talked about the tubes that were sticking into her grandfather and the blood that she saw.

Since those early days of television and videotapes, the varieties of media have multiplied. Children, at younger and younger ages, have unrestricted access to video games, iPads, smartphones, and other multimedia sources that contain violent and inappropriate content.

The issue of media exposure can be a source of contention, particularly with dads. I recently had a family seek counsel regarding their five-year-old son. He was having difficulty adjusting to kindergarten and was struggling at home. He rarely slept through the night, experienced night terrors, and regularly wanted to sleep with Mom and Dad. He became extremely anxious when Mom left to run errands or went into another room of the house. He didn't want to go to school, so getting out of the house each morning was an ordeal.

As I talked with Mom and Dad, it was apparent that the child's father was an avid gamer. He saw no harm in playing violent games in the presence of his child and sometimes even involved his son in the games because, after all, it was just "fantasy." He explained that he didn't want to raise a "mamby pamby" mama's boy, so he felt that exposing his son to these things only helped to make him more "macho." He refused to recognize that exposure to this kind of media only served to undermine his son's sense of felt safety.

The unhealthy effect of media on children's behavior has been well documented for decades. The brain does not discriminate between the real world and the virtual world. When children watch a movie or play a video game that involves a virtual reality, their brains are activated in the same way that the brain would function in a real setting. Exposing children to violent media serves only to undermine a sense of felt safety and their confidence that Mom and Dad are "big enough" to take care of them and keep them safe.

Our homes should be a haven of safety for our children. We virtually allow things to come into our living room that we would never consider exposing our children to in real life. But the effects are the same. Every minute that a child spends in front of a screen is a minute that he is not connected to a person. Research confirms that most children in America spend more time connecting to a machine than they do connecting to their parents.

Machines don't wire brains in complex ways. Machines don't impart love and a sense of felt safety. Machines don't build emotional connections that anchor and orient children to what is important in life.

Parents should serve as a child's "compass," orienting them to the world and helping them to understand what is important and what is not, what is right and what is wrong, how to behave and how not to behave. When parents abdicate this important role to different forms of media and allow fictional characters to orient a child to the world, healthy relationships are undermined.

Availability

Trust is the foundation of strong emotional connections and requires ongoing nurture and attention throughout childhood. Lieberman and Van Horn (2008) define trust as the "conviction that the parents are consistently available, 'able and willing' to protect the child from conditions that undermine the child's sense of well-being."

Being available means that we are both physically and psychologically present to the child on a consistent basis. As children move into the preschool years and they no longer require us to monitor their every move, parents can mistakenly believe that they are more independent than they really are. Though they may not need us to be physically by their side every moment of the day, they still need significant availability to meet their emotional needs. The relationship begins to shift from being primarily centered on physical closeness to one that is more centered around emotional closeness.

Physical Availability

As a culture, we have bought into the myth that "It's about quality time and not about quantity." When it comes to our preschoolers, it *is* about quantity. Quality time can't be manufactured and conjured up whenever it fits in our calendar. Quality doesn't happen without quantity.

The younger our child is, the more face-to-face time is required. It might suffice in the teen years to have a meaningful 20-minute conversation at breakfast in the course of the day, but spending only 20 minutes with my preschooler constitutes neglect.

Many have been led to believe the lie that "We can have it all." Yes, we can have it all, but not at the same time. The Scripture clearly teach that there are seasons in life. The preschool years constitute a season of life when we may need to limit our involvement in activities outside the home, especially if we are working full-time, in order to effectively meet the attachment needs of our children.

We frequently train early childhood professionals and recently met an eighty-year-old woman in a small town in Oklahoma who has been providing childcare in her home for over fifty years. Someone asked why children are so angry these days. She piped up and said, "I'll tell you why they're angry. They are angry because they never see their parents. They know they aren't important to them!" She went on to describe the changes she has seen over her fifty years of caring for children.

We encourage families where both parents need to work-full time to try to choose jobs that accommodate the needs of their family, rather than expecting children to accommodate the needs of the parents' jobs. Choosing a job with flexible hours or the ability to work from home can allow parents to be more available to their children. I have seen parents do some creative juggling with their work schedules, so children are with one of their parents for a majority of time and in childcare on a limited basis. This also may mean taking a job that isn't necessarily your dream job for a season, so as to be more available to your children in the preschool years.

Tough choices have to be made. Never have we had a parent tell us that they regretted their choice to be more available to their children. But many have said they regret the years lost to a job.

Emotional Availability

It is possible for a parent to be physically present with a child yet be emotionally absent.

Preoccupation is perhaps the worst enemy of good parenting. As our children get older and are less dependent upon us for their physical needs and moment-to-moment safety, it gets easier to become preoccupied and be emotionally unavailable to our children.

After the demanding years of infancy and toddlerhood, parents sometimes get a false sense of relief that now they can go back to doing their own thing and pursue interests that they may have set aside previously.

The importance of being emotionally available is particularly important for parents who work from home. I have met parents who have chosen to work at home. Though they may be physically present, they are emotionally checked out and preoccupied. With the fast-paced life that we all lead, preoccupation is a concern for us all.

Attunement

As our children move into the preschool years, it becomes easier to discern their most basic needs. They are able to tell us when they are hungry and thirsty or when they need to go to the restroom. But there is still much that they communicate through their behavior.

As we strive to accurately attune to and interpret the "cues" of our preschooler, it becomes more about recognizing their motives, intentions, desires, beliefs, fears, and worries. In other words, we attune to their "inner life."

The essence of attunement communicates the message that, "*I see you, I hear you, and I understand you.*" One of the ways that we communicate to our children that we truly "see them" is to speak words of encouragement and send "I notice you" messages.

Patting our children on the back and telling them how "awesome" they are only serves to create entitled and narcissistic children. There's a better way.

When we send, "I notice you" messages, we identify specific behaviors and character qualities that are desirable. For example, while spending the afternoon at the park, you notice that your five-year-old son gave up his turn on the swing so that his little sister could have a turn. On the way home from the park, you might say to him, "I noticed that you let Emily have your turn on the swing. That was a very thoughtful thing to do." Or, "I noticed that when the other boys told the new child he couldn't play with them, you offered to let him play with one of your cars. That was a very kind thing to do."

These words of encouragement let children know that we truly notice them and validate their "goodness." It also communicates in a concrete and specific way the behaviors that we value and want to encourage.

I Hear You

"Hearing" our preschooler means we "listen" to their behavior as well as their words. This can be a challenge because the thinking and, therefore, the behavior of a preschooler is very different than that of an adult. They do things that seem crazy to us but make perfect sense to them.

The other day, someone asked me what parents should do when their child has a temper tantrum. She said she has always been told that parents should ignore the child and act as if they didn't see or hear them.

The truth is that behavior is a form of communication, and all behavior conveys a message. Most temper tantrums are the result of fatigue, hunger, or overstimulation. Attuned parents recognize this and respond by giving children what they need rather than ignoring or punishing. Yelling, slapping, or ignoring a hungry, tired, or overstimulated child will only undermine emotional connections.

We've heard parents argue that to not punish a child for a temper tantrum is coddling and "giving in" to them. Meeting a child's need for hunger, rest, and comfort when overstimulated is not coddling. Most children are not able to accurately verbalize their need for food, rest, or comfort until around five years of age. Before they are capable of this cognitive capacity, they "feel" the need and demonstrate it through behavior. "Giving in" to children means that I cater to their inappropriate demands and wants.

It's important for both children and parents to learn the difference between a child's needs and wants. It is always appropriate to meet their needs, but it is inappropriate to give into their every want. When we cater to our children's every wish, we make them weak, and they will perceive us as weak. In order to feel safe, children need to know that there is someone who is big enough to take care of them and say, no when appropriate.

I Understand You

Allison Gopnik, developmental psychologist and professor at Berkley, researches the thinking of young children. She reports that when scientists measure the brain waves of preschoolers, their brain activity looks like that of an adult on a psychedelic drug! So now you know why parents are sometimes bewildered by the antics of preschool children.

Understanding means that we seek to grasp the motivations, intentions, desires, and thinking of our children.

For example, I (Barbara) was recently reminiscing with my 28-year-old daughter. She recounted an instance in which she felt misunderstood as a four-year-old. Her dad is a quadriplegic, and one of the parts of his body that doesn't work is his "thermostat." He is unable to regulate his body temperature, so in the summer, when he goes outside for any length of time, he has to be squirted with a spray bottle of water to keep him cool.

One day, a friend of ours came over to mow the grass on a hot July day. She and a friend were watching him from an upstairs window. Thinking that he looked hot, she got a cup of water, opened the screen, and poured the water on his head. This made perfect sense to her, but not to her dad. He scolded her and sent her friend home. The fact that she remembered it all these years attests to the magnitude of the emotion she felt.

After working with children for over four decades, we have come to believe that young children do their best possible thinking in any given situation. They do what makes sense to them, but that doesn't always make sense to the adult. In order to attune to the inner life of our children, we have to be able to "walk in their shoes" and look at any given situation from their perspective—not an easy task.

Understanding Big Emotions

Preschoolers experience *big* emotions. They feel what they feel very intensely. Sometimes their big emotions seem irrational and blown out of proportion, but remember you're dealing with a very different brain than that of an adult. Not many preschoolers feel things "just a little bit." For example, just today I was talking with my daughter on the phone. Suddenly I could hear commotion in the background and my four-year-old granddaughter crying. She was coloring with markers, and the red and yellow marker were bleeding together, "ruining" her picture.

A common response from adults is to minimize their angst or try to talk them out of it. Mom might say something like, "It's not that big of a deal. You can make another picture." Or, "It doesn't look that bad. Just color over it." Or, "There is no need to cry. If you want to cry, I'll give you something to cry about." These responses create shame and feelings of inadequacy in children.

But instead of reacting, we can respond in a way that communicates "I hear you, I see you, I understand." *What would that look like?* Mom might say, *"You have worked hard on that picture. It's frustrating when the markers don't work like you want them to."* I find that when children feel "heard," it is often enough to move them beyond the frustration and into problem-solving.

At the core of our being is a desire to simply be understood. That is the power of attunement. Attuning does not mean we condone the feelings. It just says, "I get where you are coming from. This is hard for you." So the next step would be to do some problem-solving and figure out what materials are needed to get the desired outcome.

Imagine your family has been looking forward all week to a family outing at the park. Unfortunately, the weather doesn't cooperate and it turns out to be a wet and dreary day. When you tell your four-year-old that the trip will be postponed, she stomps off to her bedroom and you hear stuff being thrown around the room.

So how do we attune and communicate, "I get you," while at the same time, letting her know that throwing things around the room is not acceptable? First, you would go into her room and say something like, "I know you are very disappointed because you really love the curly slide at the park. But it is not okay to throw stuff around the

106

room. Let's get it picked up, and then we can brainstorm some other possibilities of things we can do. Let me know when you are done and ready to talk."

If your child is over-the-top upset, you might have to help her calm down with a hug, a drink of water, or some other intervention that typically calms her. Then you can acknowledge her disappointment, address the inappropriate behavior, and then find something else the family can enjoy together.

Here's another common scenario, and we've all been there.

Your child is at a birthday party, and things are pretty wild and crazy. Your child is obviously getting tired and overstimulated, so you decide it is time to go home. You give your child time to wind down and tell him that he has five minutes left to play and then you will be leaving. When it comes time to leave, he loudly protests and does the "wet noodle" thing and flops on the floor crying.

If I am going to truly see, hear, and understand my child, I need to accept the fact that my child is overstimulated and has limited capacity at the moment to regulate. He has been having a great time, and who likes to stop having fun?

So instead of getting angry, I acknowledge the emotion and the desire behind the behavior. Then I employ a tactic we discussed earlier—can you guess what it is? I might say something like, *"You've been having such a good time playing with your friends, and it is really hard to stop playing when you are having fun. But it is time to go home. Would you like a piggy back ride or would you like to hop like a bunny to the car?"*

But sometimes in these situations, I can only see, hear, and understand my own embarrassment and frustration at my child's lack of obedience. My own needs prevent me from truly attuning to my child because there is too much static on the line. When I have tunnel vision and my own needs clamor for attention, I am likely to respond inappropriately, or even harmfully, to my child. This results in ruptured attunement. The child is left in a state of aloneness to deal with his own overwhelming emotions.

Unconditional Acceptance

When we attune to our children—and see, hear, and understand them—we offer them unconditional acceptance. Preschoolers are growing in their realization that they have their own thoughts, feelings, desires, preferences, and interests. As their command of the English language increases, they begin to clearly tell us what they are thinking, wanting, and feeling. When we refuse to give them ice cream before dinner, they tell us that we are mean. When we refuse to buy them a toy that they are demanding, they exclaim that they don't like us. How we respond to these declarations will set the stage for whether or not we will continue to have open lines of communication in the teenage years.

The goal is to accept their feelings, thoughts, and desires without judgment. This doesn't mean that we agree with them. And it doesn't mean that we don't express our own thoughts and opinions. Consider the following.

Three-year-old Josiah loves potato chips. He asks mom for some potato chips as she prepares dinner. Mom tells him that they will be eating soon, and eating potato chips will interfere with dinner. She offers him some carrot sticks, but he gets angry and yells, "You're mean."

She responds by saying, "Don't you talk to me that way. You are being disrespectful and rude. You are not getting any dessert tonight, young man."

What has happened here? Mom basically told Josiah that his feelings are not okay—expressing negative emotions is *not* acceptable and is judged to be "disrespectful and rude." When children's negative emotions are responded to in a judgmental way, they will, over time, repress their "unacceptable" feelings and become less in tune with their inner life. If their feelings are met with rejection, they will stop talking to us. As they get older, they won't come to us when they are having trouble with another kid at school, or when they are faced with a moral challenge as a teenager. They will be afraid of "speaking the unspeakable," and emotional connections will slowly fade.

Consider another option.

When Josiah tells Mom that she is "mean, " she might say something like this: *"I'm sorry that you feel like I'm being mean. That makes me sad. But it's my job to help you stay healthy. I want you to have plenty of room in your tummy to eat some good food that will help you grow strong."*

Mom has communicated to Josiah that she is "big enough" to handle his anger. Mom isn't going to fall apart. In fact, she's honest about her own emotions in the moment. She still loves him and wants the best for him. He has learned that he can share even his negative thoughts and feelings without being shamed.

Shame is toxic to healthy relationships. Shame causes children to feel bad about who they are. Shame causes children to withdraw and hide from us. It drives children to lie, blame others, and make excuses for their behavior. If this kind of response becomes routine

108

in the preschool years, by the time our children enter elementary school, the lines of communication will be shut down, and emotional connections will erode.

We help children feel safe when we provide appropriate and consistent limits that are lovingly and consistently applied. Appropriate and consistent limits communicate to the child, "I am strong enough to take care of you." Inconsistent and arbitrary limits undermine children's trust in our ability to care for them.

But *how* we enforce and apply the limits we establish is critical. Limits that are harshly enforced and discipline that is humiliating will undermine any sense of felt safety in our presence. Rules without relationship will only alienate. With the growing independence and capabilities of the three-to-five year-old child, there will be plenty of opportunities to set limits, so let's look at how to do this in ways to create and maintain a sense of felt safety.

Responding to Misguided Behavior

With increased mobility and independence, the preschooler is now able to do things that just a few short months ago he was unable to do. They can open doors, drawers, and cabinets. They can use small tools such as scissors, markers, and crayons. Their drive to test and figure out how their world works can lead them into situations that, at first glance, may look like disobedience and defiance but is really a form of exploration.

For example, a three-year-old who is just learning how to use crayons gets caught up in the moment and draws a picture on the wall of his bedroom.

If a parent interprets the behavior as willful defiance, he is likely to respond in a punitive way and yell, put the child in time out, or take away the crayons. The parent may say something like, "You know better than that!" "What were you thinking?" "Now you've done it! You've ruined the wall." How we respond to our children in moments such as these will either weaken or strengthen the emotional bond. Harsh discipline is one of the primary ways that parents erode strong emotional connections with preschoolers. Consider the two possibilities.

Three-year-old Josiah has discovered the pleasure of using crayons. Throughout the day, he sits at the little table in his room and enjoys coloring. One afternoon, he is particularly enthralled with his creations, and his

109

scribbling overflows onto the wall, just as Dad walks in and sees what he is doing. With a look of glee, Josiah says, "Look Daddy. It's a spider."

Dad grabs the crayon from Josiah's hand and yells, "You know better than that! Now look what you have done! You've ruined the wall!" Dad takes the basket of crayons and puts them in the top of the closet and tells Josiah he can't have them anymore. Terrified at his father's outburst, Josiah begins to cry, runs to his bed, and buries his head under the pillow. Dad stomps out of the room muttering about how he going to have to clean the wall. For the rest of the evening, Josiah avoids Dad. When it is time to go to bed, Mom tells Josiah to go say goodnight to Daddy. Josiah shakes his head and clings to Mom's leg.

Josiah's "misguided behavior" was motivated by experimentation. Sometimes children simply lose themselves in an activity or try things just to see what would happen. Experimentation behavior is characteristic of preschoolers. In this case, it is likely that he got caught up in the joy of coloring, and his canvas extended to the wall. This doesn't mean that the behavior is excused or thought to be "cute" and simply laughed at. But it does mean that a parent needs to respond in a way that helps the child learn appropriate boundaries while preserving emotional connections. Let's consider a different scenario.

Dad walks into the room and sees Josiah coloring on the wall. Dad is startled but quickly discerns what is happening, and very kindly but firmly says, "Whoa, bud! Not on the wall. Put the crayon in my hand." Josiah stops in his tracks and looks expectantly at Dad. He slowly puts the crayon in Dad's hand and Dad says, "Hey, buddy, I know you love to color, but it is not okay to color on the walls. Crayons stay on the paper. Let's get a rag and some cleaner, and you can help me wipe it off." Dad and Josiah clean off the wall, working side by side. When they are finished, Dad and Josiah enjoy a few moments of coloring together.

In this vignette, Dad addresses the behavior in a way that is constructive and preserves the emotional safety and connection between himself and Josiah. He acknowledges Josiah's intent—he loves to color. He states the expectation: "We don't color on the walls. Crayons stay on the paper." And he holds Josiah accountable for his actions by having him help clean the wall. He reconnects by taking time to color with Josiah. As they work together Dad reinforces the importance of keeping the crayons on the paper.

But we know what you're thinking. *What if the next day Josiah does the same thing again?* There are several ways that you can preserve the connection and address the behavior. It is always helpful to address

110

behavioral issues from a problem-solving perspective. Dad might say something like, "Hey, bud, it seems that you are having trouble keeping your crayons on the paper. Do you have any ideas on how we can help you manage that?"

It is likely that Josiah will look at Dad with a "deer in headlights" look the first time this happens. Dad can offer some possibilities. "Maybe it would be helpful if you color at the kitchen table, so we can keep an eye on you and remind you to keep the crayons on the paper." Or, "Maybe you will only be able to color when Mom or Dad can sit down with you and help you remember to keep your crayons on the paper."

So, now let's assume that Josiah agrees to color at the kitchen table, but when Dad reminds him that he can't color in his room, Josiah loudly protests. Dad might say something like, "It seems that coloring at the table is too hard for you today. We will put the crayons up and try again tomorrow."

It is likely that Josiah's protest will get even louder. So Dad once again resonates with his desire to color. "I know, bud. You love to color, but you can only color at the kitchen table so we can help you to remember to keep the crayons on the paper. We will try again another day."

Dad draws Josiah close and kindly but firmly says, "No crayons today." Then he comforts, holds, and gives him two choices of two other activities to do.

Building strong connections does not mean that we coddle, give in, or let children get away with inappropriate behavior. (We'll address discipline in a later chapter.) When we do not hold them accountable and we sidestep the issue to avoid a meltdown, we make children weak. Children are looking for someone who is "big enough" to take care of them. When we are too psychologically weak to hold them accountable, we actually erode strong connections.

Providing instruction and correction in a way that strengthens attachment is a process and not a moment in time. Instant obedience is not the goal. Instant obedience can be obtained through power, control, reward, punishment, and coercion—but it will happen at the expense of the connection. These forms of behavior management are a fear-based approach to parenting, and fear obviously undermines the felt safety we want to create with our children.

You'll find that as the connection grows, behavior challenges will become less frequent.

Err and Repair

So what do we do when we mess up and fail to attune? The good news is we don't have to be perfect. When we fail to *"see, hear, and understand"* our children—and recognize the rupture—we go to our child to apologize, ask forgiveness, and make repair. I am continually amazed at the forgiveness of children, and you will be, too. They are quick to forgive.

Dr. Curt Thompson, in his book *Anatomy of the Soul,* states that when we "err and repair," the brain actually grows new neurons! Isn't it amazing that God knew we were going to mess up and He made a way to redeem our shortcomings?

When you err, don't shy away from repair. You and your child will grow as a result.

Connecting Through Playful Engagement

Play and playful engagement continue to be an important avenue of connection for preschoolers. Following their lead in play is important as it validates children's interests and abilities. During the preschool years, children develop strong preferences for certain kinds of play. Some love dramatic or pretend play. Others love to construct things with blocks, Legos®, and Tinkertoys®. Children with an artistic bent gravitate toward paint, markers, and play dough.

It's our job as a parent to look for the natural inclinations of our child and provide encouragement and opportunities for them to pursue things that are of interest.

Sometimes a parent's own unfulfilled desires get in the way of truly seeing children and appreciating their uniqueness. Some see their children as extensions of themselves and steer them into activities for which the children have no desire or talent. These children live their lives trying to stifle their desires in an effort to earn the love of their parents.

Sports have become a national obsession. Just sit on the sidelines of any Little League ball game, and you can easily identify the parents who are living vicariously through their children. They yell and belittle every mistake their child or their coach makes. We've all seen the child in the outfield who would rather chase butterflies than baseballs.

Ideas for playful interaction:

- Play board games: Candyland; Chutes and Ladders; Heigh-Ho Cherry-O; Guess Who?; Hungry, Hungry Hippos; Go Fish.
- Make play dough or slime together.
- Color or paint together.
- Take a walk and look for bugs, birds, or interesting rocks.
- Throw a blanket over the kitchen table to make a tent, and eat lunch with the kids there.

Reflections

Think of an instance in your own childhood when you felt misunderstood by your parents. How did it make you feel? What do you wish they had known?

Think of an instance in your childhood when your parents clearly communicated, "I see you, I hear you, I understand you." How did it make you feel? How did you feel toward your parents?

Application

Watch for behaviors that might not make sense to you at first glance. Put yourself in your child's shoes, and brainstorm why this particular behavior might make sense to your child.

- Look for a way to "hold your child in mind."
- Send an "I notice you . . ." message to your child every day.
- Play a board game with your child.
- Invite your child to help you cook dinner.

Chapter Eight

Nurturing Relationships with Your School-ager: Staying Connected While Apart

We define "school-age" as six through twelve years old, as these are the typical ages of children in first through sixth grades. This period of development can also be considered middle childhood.

This period of development is usually the first time children begin to devote time and energy in relationships with people other than their parents. For many children, school is the first environment where substantial time is spent outside the home. New relationships with teachers and friends will challenge them to exercise their growing sense of security.

School-agers now begin to recognize new areas of interest and branch out to try new things, as their exposure to other children and teachers brings additional information into their lives. How Mom and Dad respond to the children's budding sense of self-understanding will either strengthen their connection or slowly erode their emotional ties.

Our children are ultimately not our own. They belong to the God who made them. They are only on loan to us for the years we have on earth, and our job is to help them discover the purpose for which they were made. We are all created to enjoy healthy relationships.

We know from scientific research that we're all uniquely created with our own individual genetic makeup, and many of our strengths and weaknesses have biological origins.

Availability

Being aware of our child's temperament (quiet and reserved or active and engaging) and tending to these individual traits helps a child prepare for transitions beyond the family. A parent's availability is key at this pivotal moment in the child's life. Guidance in discerning the child's emotional state as they stretch and exercise the skills necessary for this shift is important to assess. Supporting them through this time will require your presence and focus.

Unlike the previous years of constant physical availability, the years in middle childhood are characterized by play dates, extracurricular activities—and later, being at home for shorter periods without adult supervision.

Routines

For the early school-ager, the development of routines is imperative. They are now balancing their world at home, along with expanded expectations outside the house. In order to guide them to best handle multiple challenges, Mom and Dad need to provide school-age children structure through a predictable daily routine.

Taking care of physical needs avoids undue emotional distress. Regular bed and wake times will provide kids regulation that enables them to be well-rested and ready for the new demands of school. Consistent meal and snack times help children avoid drops in blood sugar and prevent hunger from preoccupying their behavior.

Routines enable a child to feel safe when the world around them is changing.

Children are provided a sense of security when they know what to expect day to day. If their environment has a rhythm of transitions that help them to feel rested, nourished, and prepared, children are equipped with basic necessities that help them achieve ever-increasing goals and skills at school.

For the child who lives in a chaotic, unstructured environment, preoccupation with feeling hungry or irregular sleep conditions can inhibit her development. Children who aren't offered safe and comforting conditions at home are ill-prepared to function in the larger setting of school.

Allison had a fitful night of sleep. The usually feisty eight-year-old wakes to her mother stroking her hair and gently rubbing her arms, bringing her gently into the day. Mom says, "I know last night was a rough night for you. Let's take some extra time this morning to help you get ready for school." Allison whines the she doesn't feel good. They rock while Mom reads Allison a story. Mom then offers to make her breakfast while she dresses. Mom sits with Allison while she eats, and they talk about what will happen after school. Mom talks about maybe going to the park together and then coming home for some quiet time to help her rest after a hard night. She asks Allison, "What sounds good for dinner?"

Mom's slow approach is sensitive to Allison's rough night. She approaches the day and adapts to Allison's lower-than-usual activity level. Mom attunes to Allison's need for an approach of lowered intensity, and sets the pace by making unhurried transitions that morning. She concentrates on being more tactile, stopping for moments along the way to give hugs, eye contact, and gentleness that signal her appreciation for Allison's loss of sleep and less-than-chipper mood. Allison leaves for school with a feeling that Mom cares and understands how she feels.

If I wake my child tenderly, allowing entry into the morning to be comforting and unhurried, I set the stage for a great day, both away and together. When I have assembled what we will have for breakfast and healthy snacks, prepared backpacks, and laid out school clothes the night before, I'm ahead of the game before the family goes their separate ways.

The child with a temperament that is slow to warm up to new situations may need more help to master increasing hours away from home. More time may be needed in the morning to enthusiastically prepare this child by reviewing what class comes after math, and to help order the day in her mind.

One of the issues we often see in families is the tendency to overschedule. After the rigors of a day filled with learning, children need time to let their minds wander into imaginative play. This, coupled with physical activity to compensate for hours of focused attention-giving at school, helps children to let go of stress in their day. Remember that play is the language of children, and they need to learn to develop positive strategies to deal with stress. All too often, children either return home to screen time of some sort or rush off to structured extracurricular activities.

Many times, when you ask your child, "How was school today?" you hear pat answers of "fine" resulting in a dead-end to connection. If you model sharing examples of "Tell me something funny that happened today," or "Let me tell you what happened to me today," you open the door to an attachment-based transition between school and home.

Sports, music lessons, and pursuits of interest to the child are often replacements for time with parents—they can become a substitute babysitter. Not to say these aren't important activities; identifying and nurturing a child's gifts helps them grow into confident teens who exercise their strengths. Care needs to be taken not to rush children into too many extracurricular pursuits too soon.

Transition into school needs to be guided by the parent, discerning their child's adjustment to the new daily tasks.

Emotional Availability: Holding You in Mind

As families begin to spend more hours apart, it's important to communicate to your child that you "hold them in mind" or, in other words, you think about them when you're not together.

This is especially important for the parent who travels or is deployed in military service.

It can be something as simple as buying their favorite gum at the store, picking up a rock on your morning walk to add to their rock collection, or baking their favorite cookies while they're at school.

Here are some other ideas:

- Write notes of encouragement on their napkin that goes in their lunch.
- Write a note of encouragement on the bathroom mirror with window markers.
- When you go out of town for a longer stay, leave notes around the house in strategic places.
- Video chat when you are on business trips.
- Ask your child to look after a favorite bracelet, watch, or other piece of jewelry while you're gone.
- Spray a cotton ball with your perfume, so a child can "smell you" in your absence.
- Send a postcard.

118

We all need to feel our value and worth to those who love us. Attachment is built from many looks, touches, and gestures that communicate our care to our children and family. Leaving a child with feelings that you are lovingly holding them in mind before, during, and after times together is the glue that holds us in their thoughts.

Attunement

Research substantiates that children who have a secure attachment with parents are more successful in areas of social skills, increasing verbal skills, and exploration of new areas of interest. If children have experienced stability and security in their homes, their minds are free of anxiety as they experience new situations. If a child has come from a home that has been anxious, dismissing, or fearful, the child will expect the same conditions in his new environment.

Imagine the difference of parenting strategies in which a parent has prepared the child with school visits, met with the teacher, obtained school supplies, and rehearsed their daily schedule—versus a child who is thrust into a new environment with none of this preplanning.

In preparation for school, a parent is able to observe the child in each of these new circumstances and help the child begin to verbally identify areas of concern. Coupled with the earlier parenting skills of "*I see you, I hear you, I understand*," the parent is now able to help their child identify how to verbally express needs.

The need for attunement with the young school-ager is important, as the time apart is filled with new social demands, learning challenges, and rigors of a new schedule. In middle childhood, the child is learning to balance social and academic expectations with a myriad of emotions.

In today's society, a parent's availability and attunement to help make sense of this new diversity of people, experience, and corresponding value systems has never been more important.

Felt Safety

As children move into the elementary school years, they are exposed to many changes and new adventures. The time they spend away from Mom and Dad increases, and peers take on new importance. They begin to develop an awareness of their own strengths and weaknesses—what they're good at, and what they aren't. For the first time, our children need to carry their sense of safety with them, in our absence.

119

Because of their first separations from us for a substantial portion of time, it's important at day's end to assess their internal sense of emotional safety. How do they feel about themselves in this new context, and are they able to discuss their successes, fears, frustrations, and anxieties?

In working with many parents over the years, as well as practicing with my own children, I found it to be very important to "get in sync" with one another when returning from school and work. When they were little, lap time to physiologically and physically regain connection, while sharing a snack, talking about the day away from one another, and planning for the evening, helped us to "get on the same page."

Contrast this with days when I was out of sync. I hurried in to think about what was for dinner. The girls went their separate ways, staying in the emotional space they came home in. Dad came through the door, and we chased feeling connection throughout the night. Dinner was spent decompressing, but we hadn't unloaded our stress in a connected way. Not having come together in a meaningful way to take a mutual "deep breath" and share our individual emotions and experiences, we were left with a disconnected sense of family unity.

Fostering connection takes intentional focus to take stock of our children's thoughts and feelings—and our own emotions. Sometimes parents and children wander through their days without making meaningful connection. Before I forge ahead with planning what comes next day to day, attuning to the present emotion my child is feeling will help me know when to stop and refuel.

"Before you go out and play, can I have a hug?" "Is there anything at school that upset you today?" "I haven't looked into your eyes today, and I want to stop and check in with you."

By holding your child, you can sometimes feel the release of pent-up energy. Encouraging deep breaths and slowly releasing together, you can help your child learn some simple ways to let go of stress.

Teaching your child to be aware of how they hold tension in their bodies develops an awareness of how they manifest stress. Sweaty palms, tension in neck, headaches, or tight calves or arms can help kids begin to identify the connection between mind and body. Stretching techniques, massage, rocking, and holding one another build strong connection between you and your child.

Stopping to assess, rest, and connect strengthens families.

Allowing and Encouraging Individuality

When we carefully nurture our children's budding strengths, we provide them with encouragement and opportunities to develop the

120

gifts they've been given. In doing so, the emotional ties to our children are strengthened.

Many parents see qualities in their children that remind them of themselves. In their desire to relive or recreate their own experience, parents may push their children to excel in areas of their own desire and not their children's interest.

Our children are not extensions of ourselves, and it's not our place to impose our own expectations on them.

Many parents vicariously live through their children. The dad who never achieved his dream of being a football star coerces and manipulates his son to try out for the football team. Even though his son would rather play drums in the band, he complies to avoid his father's ridicule and finds himself doing something that he hates. He's afraid of his father's response if he quits the team and endures the drudgery of playing.

By the time children enter middle school, it's important they identify at least one thing they enjoy or are good at.

Much of their social life in adolescence revolves around their extracurricular interests. The volleyball players hang out with other volleyball players. The band members hang out with other band members. The child who has no identified interest often flounders, and school is a miserable place to be without friends.

Touch

As children move into the later elementary years, it is important to be sensitive to your child's normal but sometimes disappointing aversion to affectionate touch in public.

For some children, especially boys, it is no longer "cool" to give Mom a hug at the door of the classroom. They may be perfectly willing in the privacy of the car, but not in front of their friends.

At this stage, they are more accepting of "play." These are the years you can nurture a love of outdoor pursuits and strengthen attachments with family activities that encourage movement, exercise, positive habits, and time spent together.

Here are ten ways to continue to nurture your school-ager through the power of touch:

1. Hugs, high fives, fist bumps, and handshakes
As you come and go throughout the day, make a habit of physical connection whenever you leave and come back.

2. Hair-brushing rituals
There aren't too many people who don't enjoy having their hair brushed. Making this a routine before bedtime can be relaxing and a fun way to connect.

3. Back rubs and massages
The old saying, "different strokes for different folks" is literally true. Children often enjoy back rubs before bed, after doing homework, while waking up in the morning, or whenever they're stressed. Some just like their legs massaged, some only their arms, others just their back.

A knowledgeable massage therapist can train parents in massage techniques specific to a particular sport that child might play. A sports massage focuses on specific muscles that are involved in a particular activity and provides a "warm up" before playing.

4. Manicures
Young girls enjoy having their hands massaged and getting a manicure with Mom. Even little girls can participate. Just use water-based nail polish that easily washes off.

5. Musical games
Children enjoy singing songs such as "skinnamarink-a-dink-a-dink" while creating hand clapping rhythms with Mom and Dad.

6. Do the motions to "Eensy, Weensie Spider" on your child's back or as they go to sleep, "apply makeup or a superhero mask" while gently tracing eyebrows, cheekbones, and lips.

7. Playful chants

Here is a little chant my granddaughter loves:

Around the world in 80 days (Make a circle on your child's back)

X marks the spot (make an X on your child's back)

Comma, comma, comma, question mark (Make three commas & a question mark)

Spiders crawling up your back (Create a spider's crawl with your fingers)

Bite, bite, bite (Gently pinch the shoulders)

Tight squeeze (Gently squeeze the rib cage)

Cool breeze (Blow on their neck)

Now you have the shivers (Run you finger up their spine).

8. Rough-and-Tumble Play

Boys love rough-and-tumble play, and so do many girls who are temperamentally bent for heightened levels of activity. This boisterous form of play has been shown to help children learn to read nonverbal cues and learn to self-regulate.

This play is also an important way males bond. And dads, you need to win. Rough-and-tumble play sends a primitive message to a child that "I'm big enough, and strong enough, to take care of you."

But rough-and-tumble play can get out of hand and can become abusive. Always honor the child's request to stop play when the child has had enough. To continue tickling or playfully wrestle with a child when they've indicated they're done will cancel the benefits of the experience.

9. Do the following motions on your child's back while saying the words.

The sun is brightly shining in the sky. (Make a sun on your child's back with your finger.)

The wind is gently blowing through the trees. (Swish your fingers back and forth.)

Clouds begin to move across the sky. (Swish your palms back and forth.)

Rain drops begin to gently fall. (Gently tap your fingers all over the child's back.)

The rain begins to fall faster and faster (Vigorously tap all of your fingers on your child's back.)

The wind blows harder and harder. (Vigorously move your palms across your child's back.)

The thunder begins to roar. (Gently pound your fists across your child's back.)

The lightning flashes in the sky. (Zigzag your finger across your child's back.)

The rain begins to stop. (Slow down the pace and intensity of the raindrops.)

The wind begins to slow. (Slow down the swishing of your palms.)

The rainclouds move across the sky. (Lightly move your palms across your child's back.)

The sun begins to shine. (Make a sun.)

And a rainbow appears in the sky. (Make a rainbow on your child's back with your fingers.)

10. Piggy back rides, horseback rides, and shoulder rides.

The need for touch is so critical that when we fail to give it to our children in sufficient and frequent quantities, they're likely to look for it in ways that may not be appropriate. This is especially true for preteens and adolescents.

Often dads begin to pull away from their daughters as they reach adolescence and feel awkward showing affection toward them. Your child may suddenly avoid the goodnight embrace or pull back to a less intrusive form of touch. Dads can still communicate affection by touch such as a hand on the shoulder or a pat on the forearm.

A girl needs to spend consistent time with her father, so she has a healthy picture of how she should expect to be treated by a man, and to know what healthy boundaries are in regard to touch.

Playful Engagement of Your School-ager

Many children this age love jokes and word play. Being able to think more abstractly, they enjoy figuring out embedded meaning and looking for pictures hidden in a larger page, like *Where's Waldo* and *Hidden Pictures*. Sometimes spontaneous playful interaction may emerge that becomes an important family ritual.

A few years ago, we had a ten-year-old foster son living in our home. I knew I needed to navigate this issue of touch very carefully. It's hard to wrap your mind around what it must be like for a preteen to suddenly be living in the home of a virtual stranger. About two weeks after he came to live with us, he was preparing to go upstairs for the night. As he walked by me, he playfully poked me in the arm and said, "Poke."

I responded with a playful karate chop to his upper arm and said, "Chop."

He looked at me with a puzzled look.

"Oh, you know," I said, "Poke-chop!" It took a few seconds for him to get it, and he started laughing. This goofy little game became an important attachment ritual throughout his stay and brought a moment of laughter to some tense situations.

Some of the other suggestions for playful engagement with middle schoolers:

- Play board games such as Sorry, Monopoly, Chinese Checkers, Chess, or Yatzee.
- Teach your child a craft such as sewing, carpentry work, or cake decorating.
- Plant a garden or do yard work together.
- Go camping.
- Take a walk or bike ride.
- Plat catch with a baseball or football.
- Play Frisbee, badminton, croquet, or other yard games.
- Cook together.
- Watch a movie or TV show together and discuss.

Instead of viewing preschool, kindergarten and beyond as a time when nurture and play is "outsourced" to teachers, make the most of this amazing season in your child's growth.

Physical Changes

As children begin to physically develop in later stages of middle childhood, they begin to experience changes that will identify them as preadolescent. This is the time when secondary sex characteristics begin to emerge. Research has determined that girls begin to develop breast buds and exhibit pubic hair and boys develop testes and pubic hair as early as age eight, depending on race—with nearly all girls developing these physical changes by age twelve, and boys developing a few years later. Girls average 3.5 inches of growth in height between ages ten and twelve, while boys can experience growth of 4.5 inches in a year's time a few years later.

With these dramatic changes in appearance and corresponding emotion, parents need to be equipped to prepare the child for these transitions—and their associated feelings. If parents have established positive patterns of communication with their children, proactive conversations around sensitive issues will follow as a matter of course. For parents who don't know where to start, arm yourself with information about talking with your preteen about sensitive topics. The need to talk about difficult topics will only increase as your child grows into the teen years.

Self-care begins to be a priority as Mom and Dad begin to help the developing child learn to take care of all the tasks in which parents have previously been a part. Showering and/or bathing begins to be an individual matter, as the preteen develops physically and has an increasing desire for privacy. The establishment of routine aids this transition if the child has already been taught a time for health care issues within the context of the family.

Challenging Behavior and Emotion

With physical changes, feelings of uncertainty and pressure to measure up to expectations of others are great. This is a period where peer-group pressures come into play, and Mom and Dad need to continue discussions of being true to self and the values they have instilled.

Kids benefit from applications of Scripture—concepts of grace and judgment—better than a legalistic approach to do's and don'ts. Serving as an example of these concepts will speak more to your children than anything you say.

Because the preteen begins to invest more time apart from parents, the stability of the home has never been more important. When Mom and Dad provide a home conducive to entertaining the child's friends,

Mom and Dad have the ability to positively impact their child's sphere of influence. Your ability to form relationships of play, nurture, and encouragement with their friends promotes your values and beliefs as you support them—both as individuals and in their relationships with your child.

Your child's developing relationships outside of the family affect from whom they will seek to receive affection. With kids' previous reliance on attachments to parents, stronger ties now shift to peers and adult influences outside the family. Your child will begin to reorient himself to the interests and values of the peer group. This influx of new ideas and increasing view of how others live will expose your child to different views and beliefs.

This is also a time when kids are subject to feeling shame and guilt—and experience, often for the first time, rejection by others. It can be a fierce time of insults and put-downs as children begin to feel "not good enough" in comparison to ever changing standards of peers.

Teach your child effective communication skills and the differences between aggressive, assertive, and passive behavior. Children can be savagely mean with aggression and bullying, both verbally and physically. Helping children learn to assert themselves by expressing themselves directly but without expressing hurt toward others, gives them skills to confidently share feelings with peers. Aggressive people speak in ways that put others down or express their views in an intimidating manner. Passive people don't express their feelings at all or may agree just to keep peace.

Many children react to mean behavior of others by withdrawing and passively stuffing emotion, which fuels increasing feelings of anger. When parents know that bullying is taking place, directly or through social media, it is important to get involved. Talking with school officials and meeting with parents of the child who is initiating the bullying is important—not to accuse but to model how adults confront and effectively deal with conflicts of emotional safety head on.

With the older middle-schooler, it's important to remain open to discuss all topics without slamming the door if some are controversial. Every generation has its challenges, and the wise parent is not afraid to interpret their beliefs in the context of new issues. To have areas that are off-limits to discuss sometimes makes them all the more interesting for your child to explore or experience. If your children don't get information from you, they will get it elsewhere. Asking kids what they know about different topics allows you some context about what information they may be after.

"Rules" for your child should be broad, but encompass the kind of behavior you would like to see, and should set expectations on developing positive character. Instead of having a litany of "don'ts"— don't interrupt, don't leave your dirty clothes in the bathroom, don't leave the house with your bed unmade, focus on general character qualities such as "be responsible, respectful, and fun to be with" as noted in the parenting philosophy of researchers Cline and Fay.

For example, you can say, "I feel frustrated when I constantly find your dirty clothes all over the bathroom floor. Be respectful of others and put them in the hamper. Let's work together to create a happy home." Statements such as this demonstrates ownership of your own emotions, targets the specific behavior that is undesirable and links it to a broader character quality. The desirable behavior is identified and linked to the positive outcome of working to create a happy home.

Another example is when Mom says, "I feel frustrated when you ignore my repeated requests to take out the trash, and I'd like you to stop playing and finish your chore. Then you can get back to having fun." If the child continues to procrastinate, offer two yeses, just as you would with the toddler. Your child is learning and you are the teacher. Take this opportunity to offer to walk with him to complete the chore, or he can go himself. Rather than getting into a controlling battle of wills and disrupting the relationship, you can accompany your child to model completion of the chore. Does this action sound like the child has "won" in that situation? Avoiding a rupture in the relationship, even momentarily, is worth the time—and models how quickly a responsibility can be resolved. Helping a child get started in chores such as cleaning up their room can replace the "do it or else" messages and teach self-starting behavior.

Constantly nagging your child with, "don't do this and don't do that" is discouraging and can undermine any desire for compliance. One way to hold yourself accountable is to ask, "How would I respond if my husband or boss made this statement to me?" We say things to children and interact with them in ways that we would never consider with an adult.

As mentioned in a previous chapter, "do-overs" is an effective tool that works with children of all ages. Before having your child engage the "do over" you can use similar statements illustrated above. "I get frustrated when you constantly interrupt me while I'm visiting with my friend. This is how you get my attention in a respectful manner. Come alongside me and put your hand on my elbow and wait until I acknowledge you. Let's try that again so I can meet your needs and at the same time be respectful to my friend."

Reflections

Examine your family's daily routine. Does it nurture a structure that helps all family members organize around a predictable schedule? Could your children identify their "event planning," and do they know what general activity follows the next?

Routine establishes expectations. The child who has an idea of what follows next in their day has a freedom of thought that allows for more effective learning. When our days are consistent, we don't have to think twice about routines of daily living and what comes next in our day. This is emotionally freeing for children, who can maintain emotional stability knowing what is expected of them on a daily basis. Kids begin to function on "autopilot," and their routine becomes predictable. Children thrive with predictability, consistency, and stability. The world's influence of instability can be consistently unsettling. The influence of a stable home builds inner peace of mind.

School years can actually be a time when attachment is strengthened. And this is exactly what your child needs to stay on the right path.

Chapter Nine

Discipline as Teaching: Biblical Perspectives

My response to my child in moments of challenging behavior will have a significant impact on the strength of our emotional connection. When my child shows me his "worst self," my capacity to love unconditionally will be put to the test. If I respond harshly, I will, over time, push him away—perhaps even into rebellion. But if I don't respond at all, or if I justify and make excuses for my child's misguided behavior, I make him weak.

The manner in which I choose to discipline is crucial. As we launch into this discussion, it probably won't take you long to realize that this chapter is a little bit different than the others. It is, shall we say, a little more "academic." We are going to take a look at ancient history, the Hebrew language, and ideally challenge you to think a little deeper about the issue of discipline and children.

We're not necessarily asking you to agree with us, but hope that the perspective we present will lead you to diligently seek the Lord in deciding what is best for your children and your family.

The Definition of Discipline

Before we talk about the how-to of discipline, let's talk about "discipline" in general. Most people equate discipline with punishment.

The basic premise behind a punitive approach to discipline is the underlying notion that the bad behavior will be extinguished by attaching something negative to the action. *When my child disobeys or displeases me, I take away a privilege, isolate the child in time out, spank, or "ground" him from doing something he enjoys.* In other words, "I make you feel bad in order to be good."

This doesn't make sense from a logical perspective much less a biblical one, does it?

Let's look at the true meaning of discipline. The word itself comes from the word *disciple*, which is someone who is a follower of the teachings of another. The greatest example of true discipleship would be Jesus and his crew of twelve. He basically said to them, "Come and let me show you the way; let me show you how to live a life that is pleasing to God. Follow me and my example." Jesus embodied the kind of person He wanted His followers to become.

When I apply this definition of discipline to parenting, I have to ask myself, "Am I the kind of person I want my child to follow? Can I truly say to my child, 'Come follow me. Watch me and imitate me. Do as I do as well as do what I say'"?

If we take Jesus' example seriously, the responsibility is undeniable. Jesus discipled His motley crew of twelve, and others who followed—including many women—through example and instruction and correction as they did life together. But how do we effectively do this with our children?

What is the "Bible Approach" to Discipline of Children?

We receive many inquiries from young parents who want to raise their children well and in accordance with Scripture. The issue of spanking inevitably arises, as this form of punishment has been widely embraced by Christian churches and organizations for decades. A quick search on the internet will reveal a variety of positions on spanking put forth by different organizations claiming to have *the* biblical approach.

Some of the positions and practices of these organizations are troubling given both research into biblical teachings and what we know from child development regarding the impact of fear-based approaches to discipline.

Among the churches and organizations who publish their position on spanking, there is a great deal of similarity in thought::

- The primary age for spanking is between fifteen months and ten years of age. Spanking during this time will prevent or soften the rebellion of teens.
- Parents are commanded in Scripture to be diligent in spanking.
- Parents should only spank on the buttocks.
- Spankings should hurt but should not leave any marks. If it doesn't hurt, it really isn't discipline.
- The instrument used to spank should be a wooden spoon.
- Limit the number of swats to two.
- Parents should not spank in anger.

Perhaps you've heard these and even have come to believe that these are axioms derived from Scripture.

Is it true that the Bible clearly demands parents diligently spank their children? Does it really say we should use a wooden spoon? Let's take a look at what the Scripture actually says and apply accepted principles of biblical interpretation to what we find.

The Role of Corporal Punishment in Scripture

The Bible's teaching on corporal punishment is probably the best-kept secret in the Christian community. I have never heard a pastor preach on the topic, nor do I ever expect to. But the truth is, the Scriptures have a great deal to say about physical punishment that is likely to be a bit of a shock to us all.

We also need to understand something about the culture in which the Scriptures were written to understand the intent of the writings. While we strongly believe that the truth of Scripture—and nature of God—is unchanging, there are instances where an understanding of culture is important.

To clarify: beatings, floggings, and whippings were common practice in ancient culture. It was a widely accepted form of punishment for children, slaves, fools, and Torah violators. In Jewish culture, children would be included in all of these categories, so any reference to any one of these groups would apply to children. So let's dive in.

1. Does the Scripture indicate that the optimum time frame for spanking is between fifteen months and ten years of age?

Before we look at the specific Scriptures that can answer this question for us, we first need to understand some things about the Hebrew language. It is a very precise language. Where we have one word to indicate a concept in English, the Hebrew language might have five words identifying specific nuances of a more general word. It is the same with Greek—the language of the New Testament.

During my years in seminary, and in my own personal Bible study, I (Barbara) loved digging deep to understand the nuances of meaning of the Hebrew and Greek language. For example, where we read the word *God* in the Old Testament, there are many different Hebrew names used to indicate a specific aspect of His character. Where we read the word *love* in the New Testament, there are actually four different words in Greek describing different kinds of love.

But in all my years of study I have never heard anyone address the fact that the word *child* or *son* in Hebrew actually has eleven different words, each one denoting a particular period of development in the life of a child (Martin, online 2018). To clearly understand the meaning of a passage using the word *child*, we must know which Hebrew word is used.

Theologians spend enormous amounts of time dissecting words to accurately communicate theological concepts. Why is there not the same kind of attention given to passages regarding children? Why do we blindly accept ideas associated with parenting and the discipline of children without giving these thoughts the same rigorous attention that we give other theological concepts?

The Hebrew language is full of word pictures that are sensory-rich and help us to comprehend important truths. And so it is with the various words that are translated into English as "child" or "son." Let's take a look (Martin 2006):

- *Ben* and *bath* are general terms that are used to designate a son, a daughter, or a child of any age.
- *Yeled* and *yaldah* are terms used to refer to a newborn male and female, respectively. The term literally means "the one who came from the giving of birth."

134

- *Yonek* is a term to identify a child who receives nourishment only from the mother's breasts. No sold food is taken. In Jewish culture this would be the period from birth until around twelve months.
- *Olel* denotes a child who is still nursing but is taking in nourishment from other solid food sources. In Jewish culture the time is weaning is three years of age so this would typically indicate a child between 12 and 36 months (pg. 23).
- *Gamul* refers to a child who has completed nursing which, in Hebrew culture, would be between three and four.
- *Tapha* refers to a child clinging to its mother, or a child ranging beside her, which in Hebrew culture would be between four and six. This term is used forty-two times in the Bible to refer to "little children" in a universal way.
- *Elam* and the feminine term *Almah* are used to identify the period in life when a child is approaching adolescence.
- *Na'ar* and *na'arah* are the masculine and feminine terms to designate a young man or woman who "shakes off or shakes himself free." This word is used over 200 times, and generally indicates an unmarried young person that is about to "shake off" his family of origin to launch out and start their own.
- *Bthulah* is a term used to identify a young woman who is a virgin.
- *Bachur* is a Hebrew word that designates a young, unmarried male warrior and a time of life when men begin to marry.
- *Bachurah* is a Hebrew word referencing a young female at a time of life when she is ready to marry. However, this term is never used in Scripture.
- *Ish* is a term used to denote a grown man.
- *Bakar* refers to a firstborn child.

In light of the specifics of the Hebrew language, let's take a look at the most commonly used Scriptures to justify spanking and the specific word used to refer to a child.

Proverbs 13:24: *He who withholds his rod hates his* ben (generic word for child)*, But he who loves him disciplines him diligently.*

Proverbs 19:18: *Discipline your* ben (generic word for child) *while there is still hope; And do not desire his death.*

Proverbs 22:15: *Foolishness is bound in the heart of a* na'ar (and adolescent male); *the rod of discipline will remove it far from him.*

Proverbs 23:13–14: *Do not hold back discipline from the* na'ar (adolescent male); *Although you strike him with the rod, he will not die.*

Proverbs 29:15: *The rod and reproof give wisdom, But a* na'ar (adolescent male) *who gets his own way brings shame to his mother.*

According to Rabbi Martin (2018) the Rabbis of the day would assume that the more specific word *na'ar* would clarify the less specific *ben*. Therefore, the instruction given in these verses would be applied to male children over the age of ten or twelve. They would not be applied to younger children of any gender.

Another issue that we have to consider is that the Scriptures address the issue of corporal punishment with regard to slaves, fools, and those violating the law. In the Hebrew culture, children of all ages would be included in these identified groups. In Deuteronomy 25:1–3, physical beatings are indicated as a punishment for those who violate the Torah. Ancient texts indicate that physical punishment would be administered to those as early as twelve years of age as this was the beginning of adulthood (Webb 2011).

Exodus 21: 20–21 supports the beating of slaves but admonishes slave owners to not beat them to the point of death. It is well known that children were among the slave population, and there is no specific prohibition against beating a slave that is a child.

In light of the nuances of the Hebrew language, can anyone claim that the biblical approach to spanking is specifically targeted to children under the age of ten? A biblical case cannot be made to support this idea. At best, we can say corporal punishment is indicated for male children over the age of ten or twelve. But if you factor in the slave passages, no clear limitation with regard to age can definitively be stated.

2. Do the Scriptures put a limit on the number of swats to two?

Deuteronomy 25:3 limits the number of lashes for a law-breaker to forty! Nowhere in Scripture are any other limitations indicated. "Forty lashes" was the accepted form of corporal punishment, even for Jesus. Though I am glad that most so-called experts suggest limiting the number of swats to two, they cannot claim that it is biblical.

3. Do the Scriptures identify the buttocks as the preferred location for a spanking?

Never does the Bible say to strike children, slaves, fools, or Torah violators on the buttocks. In Deuteronomy 25:2 instructions are given to make the offender lie down so the lashes can be administered to the back. It is commonly understood that when people were beaten with a scourge, the leather straps would curl around the person's sides and tear the flesh along their ribcage as well. Therefore, a "biblical" spanking would be administered to the back and sides of a person.

4. Do the Scriptures put a prohibition on leaving visible marks as a result of administering a spanking?

No. When we look at the texts that put limitations on corporal punishment of slaves, we see that it only states that the slave should not be killed. He should not suffer permanent injury, and he should be able to get up within two days of having received a beating (Ex. 21:20–21).

The book of Proverbs even speaks to the positive aspects of physical wounds:

Blows that wound cleanse away evil; beatings make clean the innermost parts (Proverbs 20:30 ESV).

Though we wholeheartedly agree that spanking should never be done with such force as to leave marks on the body, an argument cannot be made that this is a "biblical" approach.

5. Do the Scriptures indicate that the instrument of corporal punishment should be a wooden spoon?

The "biblical" instrument for corporal punishment is clearly the rod (a stick) or the scourge as indicated in the five Scriptures previously quoted.

6. Do the Scriptures prohibit disciplining in anger?

There are many Bible passages indicating that God disciplines his

137

people out of anger. The call to administer corporal punishment to children out of love (and without anger) might have a positive intention, but it is not "biblical."

At the most, these assertions on the topic of spanking are merely the opinions of well-meaning people, informed (and misinformed) by their interpretation of Scripture (and mixed with tradition and folklore). To present their stance as "the biblical approach" is simply false and dangerous.

Ancient Culture

When I began looking at what the Bible actually says about corporal punishment, I was shocked.

Following the logic of many Christian leaders over the decades, does this mean that the biblical approach requires that we beat our children with a rod or whip, administer up to forty lashes to their back, punish out of anger, and make sure they can recover from their wounds within two days?

Of course not. But why doesn't the Bible clearly denounce these common practices? Let's take a look at this from another angle.

The Bible was written in particular times in history for a particular group of people whose way of life was very different than ours. The global culture in which the Old Testament was recorded was violent and brutal. There were severe penalties for not following the laws of the day. It was common practice to cut off hands, noses, ears, and even poke people's eyes out. Sumerian culture called for driving a peg through someone's mouth for stealing land. A woman that engaged in disrespectful speech toward her husband had her teeth smashed with bricks. In Babylonian culture, an adopted child who disowned his parents had his tongue cut out. A hired man who stole seed was dragged around the field by cattle. In Assyrian culture, a man who made unwanted sexual advances toward a woman would have his lower lip cut off with an axe blade (Webb 2011).

When we juxtapose what the Old Testament says about corporal punishment against the brutal backdrop of ancient culture, we see that these teachings were much less brutal and far more humane than the common practices of that time. Though we don't see a clear denouncing of ancient brutality, we definitely see a shift toward a kinder and gentler society as compared to the rule of the day.

We see a similar shift with regard to slavery. Brutality against slaves was an accepted part of ancient culture. Nowhere in the Bible is slavery denounced, and Peter goes so far as to tell slaves in the first century to "be submissive to their masters with all respect, not only to those who are good and gentle but also to those who are unreasonable" (1 Peter 2:18).

But does this mean that as Christians we should own slaves, beat them with a whip, administer forty lashes, leave visible wounds but make sure they are not injured to the point that they can't get up off the ground for more than two days? No, of course not.

Once again, the reason that mainstream Christianity doesn't practice slavery is because we have taken a redemptive approach to Scripture. Though the Bible never prohibits anyone from owning slaves, we interpret the Bible as a whole in light of the redemptive work of Christ. All people are created in the image of God and are not property to be possessed, bought, sold, or used for selfish purposes. Even though the slavery passages in scripture seem horrendous to us, they were actually significantly tempered against the backdrop of the cultural brutality of the era. There was definitely a movement toward a kinder and gentler society as compared to what was common at that time. And now in the 21st century, we have moved even further to embrace the redemptive work of Christ in denouncing all forms of slavery.

But why doesn't the Bible clearly condemn brutality, slavery, incest, the taking of concubines and other seemingly horrendous behavior? Dr. Curtis Vaughn was one of my favorite seminary professors at Southwestern Baptist Theological seminary. He addressed the Bible's silence on troubling issues by using the analogy of "leaven." Leaven is an agent that is used to make bread dough rise. It works internally, over time, to change the nature of the bread dough. The redemptive message of the gospel sometimes needs to be allowed to act as leaven, changing the culture and a given group of people from the inside out.

When we are speaking of large, massive, entrenched social structures, God is sometimes willing to live with the tension between the complete redemptive message of Christ and the reality of the current culture. It often takes generations of movement and change before the redemptive message is fully embraced (Webb 2011). It is not that God has changed or changes. It is the hardness of a person's heart that sometimes takes time for God's redeeming grace to penetrate and change us from the inside out.

So what does this have to do with spanking? We clearly see redemptive movement in the Scripture with regard to this issue. Against the backdrop of a barbaric society, we see that even in the Old Testament, the instructions on corporal punishment are tempered. Instead of cutting off noses, ears, hands, and mutilating body parts, slave owners are instructed to only beat their slaves but avoid killing them.

As we move into the New Testament, Christ ushers in a new, revolutionary social order that placed high value on children, women, and marginalized people—every human being of every age and race. In fact, when the disciples approached Him about the unruly children, He instructed them to allow them to come to Him. Jesus embraced the children and told the listeners they must become like a child if they desire to enter into the kingdom of heaven (Luke 18:17). He instructed adults to humble themselves like a child because only then would they be great in the kingdom. And He said that anyone who receives a child in effect receives Him.

Jesus also had severe warnings for those who cause a child to stumble. "It is better for him that a heavy millstone be hung around his neck and that he be drowned in the depth of the sea" (Matthew 18:6 NASV). In a world where children, slaves, and women were often objects to be possessed, controlled, and exploited, Jesus brought a message of redemption. He declared the inherent value of all human beings who are made in His image.

The overarching message of the gospel is that relationships take precedence over rules. No longer is our salvation dependent upon compliance to a set of regulations, but it is secured in a relationship with Jesus Christ, His work on the cross, and His resurrection. Truly, there is profound redemptive movement in the New Testament from a culture that devalued life to one that places high value on the lives of all.

The Meaning of the Word *Rod*

Another aspect of biblical language to consider is the meaning of the word *rod*. You've heard this word quoted as the scripture, "Spare the rod, spoil the child." The problem is, this phrase is not found in any English Translation of the Bible. It comes from a 17th-Century poem. [https://en.wiktionary.org/wiki/spare_the_rod_and_spoil_the_child]

The Hebrew culture was largely an agrarian society. Throughout the Old and New Testaments, the analogy of a Shepherd is consistently used to describe the relationship that the Lord has with his people, and the relationship that those in authority should have with the people they oversee.

King David was perhaps the most well known shepherd in the Bible. What did the rod mean to David?

The "rod and staff" were the primary tools shepherds used to carry out their job. The rod was used to protect the sheep and beat away predators. The staff was used to guide. Sheep are notorious for being easily distracted by what they see on the periphery. The shepherd used his staff to keep the wayward sheep on the desired path, headed in the right direction. The shepherd did not beat his sheep. They were his livelihood, and to run the risk of doing physical harm would jeopardize their well-being.

In Psalm 23, a passage of scripture that has brought great comfort to people over the years, David indicates that he finds a sense of pleasantness and comfort in the "rod." The word used here is "shebheT," which is a figure of speech alluding to divine guidance and care (International Standard Bible Encyclopedia).

Is There Room for Further Redemptive Movement?

Is there room for further redemptive movement to a position of "no spanking?" Yes, there is.

The stated purpose of corporal punishment in the Scriptures is to drive out folly and instill wisdom. Can we do this without spanking? Yes, we can, if we have an understanding of child development and how children learn.

We now have decades of neuroscience and research into the development of children to help us understand healthy interactions with our kids. We know that children learn new behaviors in the same way that they learn new skills.

Think about the first time you took your training wheels off your bicycle and tried to ride without them. Every ounce of concentration you could muster was focused on keeping your head and eyes in the right position, placing your hands and feet in the right spot, and maintaining your balance. You probably fell a couple of times but got back on and tried again. Maybe Mom or Dad hung on to the back of the bike and ran alongside you when you were figuring it all out.

While you were doing this, your brain was busy at work making

141

neural connections with regard to bike riding. Dr. Kadaras, author of *Glow Kids*, uses the analogy of sledding in terms of what the brain is doing when we are learning a new skill.

Imagine a fresh blanket of snow covering a hill by your house. You take your sled to the top and look out over the pristine landscape. As you slide down the hill on your first run, the runners on your sled make deep grooves in the snow. When you reach the bottom, you make your way back to the top and slide down again and again. On the second run, you follow in the tracks made the first time. Each time you go down, the grooves become more prominent and the snow becomes more packed so that your speed begins to get faster with each pass.

This is similar to learning to ride a bike. Each time you ride, your brain is establishing stronger and more complex connections. Over time, with multiple repetitions, your neurons develop a sort of insulation called myelin that allows the connections to fire faster and stronger. Pretty soon, you are riding down the street waving at your friends and popping wheelies without even thinking about it.

So it is when our children are learning new behaviors. They learn through modeling, coaching, instruction, and correction. This takes us back to the definition of discipline we discussed earlier. The very definition of the word implies discipleship—not punishment.

A discipleship approach to parenting requires that we let go of the mistaken belief that punishment is the motivating factor for changed behavior.

As stated throughout this book, the power to parent and influence behavior comes not from punishment but from the strength of the attachment relationship. Children are born with an innate desire to connect with those who love and care for them. When we look at how God designed children, we see that their very nature predisposes them to want to draw close to us for love and protection.

In Chapter 7, we reviewed the four core fears of every child:

1. Fear of abandonment. Children are intuitively aware of their vulnerability and inability to take care of themselves. Their greatest fear is to be abandoned both physically and psychologically.

2. Fear of bodily harm. We are wired by God for survival. We instinctively move away from things or people who we perceive are

142

harmful to us—both psychologically and physically. A sense of felt safety is critical for healthy growth and development at any age.

3. Fear of being viewed as a bad child. Every child wants us to believe in their "goodness." As we said in the Chapter 1 (and as God said in Genesis, Chapter 1), our goodness was declared by God even when He was fully aware that we would sin.

4. Fear of losing love. Children have a God-given desire to be loved by Mom and Dad. This innate drive is a gift to parents that needs to be carefully tended for.

What Does this Say About Spanking?

Physical punishment exploits the four core fears of children. Well-known Christian organizations specifically state that the purpose of spanking is to inflict physical pain. "It ought to hurt—an especially difficult goal for mothers to accept—and it's okay if it produces a few tears and sniffles. If it doesn't hurt, it isn't really discipline and ultimately it isn't very loving because it will not be effective in modifying the child's behavior." Yes, this is a direct quote from a popular Christian nonprofit.

If children are created with the God-given desire to move away from anything that is potentially harmful, what does that do to the parent–child relationship that we are trying to form?

Also, if after we spank them, we tell them that we love them, what kind of associations does this create in their mind? They associate love with physical pain—a dangerous association indeed.

Let's put this on an adult level. Let's say that you inadvertently bounce a check. Your spouse wants to teach you a lesson and make sure you never do it again. So, in addition to taking the bank fee out of your spending money for the month, your spouse hits you two times on the rear with a wooden spoon. Is the natural consequence of having less mad money to spend going to be a stronger deterrent to bouncing checks than the hits on the rear?

The two hits with a wooden spoon will likely only serve to alienate us from our spouse. This communicates a fundamental disrespect, and the human drive to psychologically and physically move away will only undermine the relationship.

143

Why do we think it's any different with children? Why do we think that just because they are little we can swat them with a spoon, and it won't have psychological repercussions?

The Relational Approach to Discipline

The dynamic between parents and children mirrors the relationship that we have with Christ. The more I *love* Jesus, the more I want to honor and obey Him. Consider the Scriptures below:

2 Corinthians 5:14 *For the love of Christ compels us . . .*

John 14:15 *If you love me, you will keep my commandments.*

In 1 John 4:18, *There is no fear in love; but perfect loves casts out fear because fear involves punishment and one who fears is not perfected in love.*

Why We Can't Let Go?

If we can accomplish the goal of corporal punishment—to drive out folly and instill wisdom—in a way that is not fear-based and is nonabusive, why wouldn't we? If the gospel message itself is clearly a movement from a law-based way of living to a relational way of living, why do we not embrace this with regard to the discipline of children? I think there are several reasons why Christians are reluctant to let it go.

- We were spanked as children, and we mistakenly believe that to reject this method of discipline is to reject our parents. It's a highly emotional journey to take a hard look at our own family and embrace a different way. We have to realize that doing things differently than our parents doesn't mean they are bad people or bad parents. We can reject a practice with our rejecting the people.

- We know no other methods for guidance. If we let go of spanking, we must have other alternatives. Do-overs, ignoring the no and giving two yeses, giving choices, time in, and conflict resolution are just a few of the strategies presented in this book. There are many other relational strategies that can be employed, but an exhaustive discussion is beyond the scope of this particular book.

144

- We don't want to do the hard work of a relationally based, attachment-oriented style of parenting. It demands far more from us as parents. *I can get the job done faster and easier in the short term with reward, punishment, power, control, coercion, and bribery.* The results of an attachment-based parenting model are long-term—and the significant difference becomes apparent in the teen years. Why do you think our teens are rejecting our values, leaving the church in droves, and moving away from the family?

If our approach to parenting is fear-based and built on our claim to authority rather than relationally based and built upon emotional connection, it is likely that our children will become more peer-oriented rather than parent-oriented as they move into the teen years. They will take on the look, the dress, the manner of talking, and the values of their peers. And we will lose our influence.

Let's Step Back and Consider
We recognize that a spanking is not the same thing as a beating. We're not saying that people who spank their children are bad parents. But we are saying that anyone who says that "the Bible demands that we diligently spank our children" or claims to have "the biblical approach to spanking" is promoting falsehoods. It's always dangerous when a pastor or a Christian leader claims to have *the* answer to topics that are not clearly stated in the Bible.

There are so many young parents who genuinely want to raise their children well, and "in the nurture and admonition of the Lord." To exploit a position of authority and unequivocally claim to have "the" truth is irresponsible.

In light of the journey we've taken through Scripture and the knowledge gleaned through child development, we submit to you our opinion. The Bible does not demand that we spank our children. It demands that we drive out folly and instill wisdom. It demands that we discipline (disciple) and teach our children. This certainly can be done without spanking.

Reflections

How were you disciplined as a child? Was spanking used by your parents?

Given the biblical information provided and the alternatives outlined in this book, do you feel there to be a case made for trying "noncontact" and relationally-informed means of discipline?

Chapter Ten

Connection through the Teen Years:
Give them Wings and Let them Fly

As children begin to move through early adolescence into the teen years, the strength of our parent–child relationship is clearly revealed.

There is a biological shift in the brain and body which begins to alter the thought processes of the teen. This can be a time of increased trepidation for a parent as their teen has increasing opportunity for exploration.

The teen's exploration propels him to move out into the world and establish his own individuality and purpose in life. For this reason, the practice of parenting for secure attachment, especially in earlier stages, is vitally important.

The transition into adolescence marks a period of extreme change in all areas of development. The teen experiences changes at a rapid pace, physically, emotionally, and psychologically. When preoccupations with physical appearance and increased prep time make you wish you'd built that additional bathroom, you begin to see the growing awareness of physical development.

Teens have an innate drive to connect with their peers. These relationships become increasingly influential and important—especially with those of the opposite sex. A parent who understands and expects these shifts in development is better prepared to effectively respond to changing emotion and behavior. Have you equipped your teen with information necessary to deal with issues at this stage?

Make your home a haven and place of enjoyment for your teen as well as their friends. Accepting, interactive parents attract teens and are able to model healthy connections with adults and model healthy family functioning.

Availability

"If we spend a quality hour together, we're good."

"It's important for my adolescent to do most everything on his own, to learn to be independent."

"My teen doesn't need me anymore and doesn't want me to participate in her sports and activities."

"My teen has so many friends; he's rarely at home—I'm so glad he's well-liked by so many people his age."

Nothing substitutes for time spent with our children.

We all know it to be true, but spending true quality time seems to elude us in the hectic, chaotic world in which we live. Without commitment to a predictable and consistent routine placing value on real "face time," we will be eaten up by the world's inclination toward nonstop work, nonstop movement, and never ending commitments. What are your commitments to maintaining physical and emotional connectedness with your family?

Parents often drive their child to be as independently functioning as possible, at the youngest age possible. Older teens have one foot in childhood and one in young adulthood. They are in the process of developing the self-confidence necessary to make decisions and master skills. But teens need a good sounding board to bounce off ideas in a nonjudgmental way.

Your communication needs to telegraph: "You are *safe* with me, no dumb questions or topics off-limits!"

While developmental achievements are important, being an active participant with your child as they master skills is crucial to secure attachment. How many attempts will a teen make before learning to drive? To interview for a job? To get the loving feedback of trying something new?

Developing patience in the face of challenges is a skill best initially observed by how your child watches you handle frustrations of "falling short," not immediately achieving success, and taking small steps toward your goals. How we handle ourselves during frustrating

150

moments makes a lasting impression on our children and models how to navigate new circumstances and emotions.

As a teen in later adolescence prepares to leave home, this transition will require use of all the connective techniques we outlined in earlier chapters.

Teens learn many lessons about how to handle emotions and roadblocks from the modeling, good and bad of their parents. When Mom and Dad are present to help identify realistic goals, show enthusiasm for efforts and guide decision-making, teens have both the physical and emotional support they need. Parents can help their teen by aiding them in breaking down larger goals into manageable tasks.

Yes, we hold parents to a high standard of making themselves available to model and participate positive behaviors with their children. It is the central truth of this book: if you are not available and connected to your children, they have no trust that what you say has any merit.

We can learn from traditional Native American parenting, which focuses on the developing child's ability to observe parents and elders before participation in a new task. Originating from the safety of the paddle board, attached to the parent, the child sees the world before reaching into it. As children grow into adulthood, observation is still key. Steps are displayed with multiple repetitions before "performance toward the goal" is ever attempted or expected.

For example, one morning I found myself standing at the bottom of the stairs shouting up to my fourteen-year-old daughter, "Are you up yet?!"

My approach didn't feel right. I was in a hurry, frustrated, and too lazy to walk up the stairs. I didn't like the disconnect I felt, and I vowed to make sure I took the time to walk up the stairs each morning.

Look for ways to make the routine events of the day an opportunity to connect.

Sit down at the breakfast table with your kids, even if your breakfast is a cup of coffee. Send children off to school with the memory of an affectionate goodbye. Even when they roll their eyes, know that they're rolling those memories into their connection with you.

Take a few moments with each person as they arrive home; make eye contact, greet them by name, and ask them about their day. (Remember to avoid "How was your day?" and ask specific questions instead.).

Take time to bring closure to the day with each child at bedtime. Ending the day with stories, prayers, and conversation sends them off to sleep with a sense of connection and emotional closeness.

Small moments of connection throughout the day fill a child's love tank—so in those moments of crisis or unforeseen separation and distress, their tank is not depleted with devastating consequences.

Small moments of kindness and connection reap great rewards.

Accessibility

Closely related to availability is the influence of our accessibility. During the time when a child's sense of self is evolving, there are a variety of influences to impact how a young teen thinks, acts, and feels. You want to be one of the voices in their head. When parents can tolerate, within reason, exploration in music, fashion and non-safety-related forms of self-expression while maintaining playful connection, they can influence more importantly held values and beliefs.

For example, when a child knows a parent is willing to listen to their music without reproach, ask about what draws teens to the beat, lyric or artist, parents start to know their children at a deeper level that reveals their developing personality.

One of the most alarming and insidious influences for our children is technology and screen time spent on any number of devices. Digital influences are affecting our youth in ever-increasing proportions. The amount of screen time is averaged at eleven hours daily, with the number of devices and screens available increasing that number.

It is important to evaluate the use and time spent on devices with the amount of actual interaction and activity of your teen. Use of devices has been linked to obesity, and increased time spent on pursuits which limit face-to-face contact limit important opportunities to develop interpersonal skills.

We have worked with numerous families where teens come home after school, retreat to their room only to come out to eat, and retreat again. Parents lament how much time is spent on the phone or computer, as if these are forgone conclusions to accept without their input. *As a parent of two teenage girls, we had a family rule that phones and computers were put up at a given time each night. This insures proper rest and helps teens learn to set boundaries around time spent on devices.*

Self-care is important to teach teens to pace themselves, rest when needed, and practice attempts at desired intents.

Strongly connected children can embrace their individuality without rejecting their parents. They may question the belief system and values that are a part of their upbringing, but they're able to do so without alienating their parents.

Those who have parented teens have felt at some point that alien abduction could be real. Thoughts and behaviors can be transitory at this phase. Relationships, as a result, can sometimes be just as short lived. Being emotionally accessible to help your teen deal with rejections of friends, changes in relationships, and maintaining friendships is a priority at this stage. Being present to help maintain a balance of behavior and emotion in the face of changing hormones and heightened insecurities can be difficult but is essential.

A parent can observe and help a teen regulate, meaning maintaining a balance of regular habits, and monitor moodiness, which can result from erratic schedules. The accessible parent knows to help a teen maintain continuity of routine, ensuring adequate sleep, diet, and underlying basics that allow for predictability and consistency.

Even when teens and parents don't see eye to eye, in a secure attachment, the parent has fostered a fundamental respect that allows them to continue a connected relationship. When affirmation is given for successfully holding to values, making good decisions, and acting on behalf of their own and others' best interests, teens build a positive sense of self.

As children transition from the developmental stage of middle childhood to adolescence, it's important to reassess their relative strengths and challenges. Previously developed skills from middle childhood that suggest a positive trajectory into the teen years includes the following:

• identifying specific and focused pursuits

• increasing physical coordination and strength

• beginning to form new group identities

• friendships with same-sex peers (primarily)

Accomplishments of middle schoolers are achieved mostly within the school context and can be seen from increasingly better verbal articulation of feelings with others to developing their own sense of style. When you look at your developing teen, have they made strides in these areas? What are areas in which they seem to be holding back or withdrawing from as they become more challenging? Mindful awareness of these developmental landmarks will guide the parent in terms of teaching opportunities.

Here are some other strategies to help your child make the transition into adolescence:

- keeping your teen safe
- being physically and emotionally available
- maintaining open communication,
- providing physical contact
- maintaining attunement and trust

Feeling Safe

Parents sometimes feel their teen's brain has been hijacked by an unknown entity, and that's not far from the truth. The teen's movement away from parents has both psychological and biological origins. The brain goes through neurochemical changes that, in a sense, propel them out into the world to establish their own identity. It is nature's way of preparing children to eventually launch out and establish their own family.

Daniel Siegle, in his book, *Brainstorm,* speaks of the drop in dopamine in the brain of an adolescent. Dopamine is the neurotransmitter, or relayer of messages in the brain, related to a sense of motivation and pleasure. This drop in dopamine drives teens toward "thrill seeking."

It's not unusual for teens to love fast cars, dangerous sports, and other forms of thrill seeking that increase the levels of dopamine in the brain and body. The CDC (Centers for Disease Control) identifies behaviors that contribute to unintentional injuries and violence as one of six primary risk behaviors identified as a challenge to adolescents.

For these reasons, it is important to assess a teen's ability to relate cause and effect—asking herself, "Do I feel like what is being proposed by others will keep me safe? What risks are involved in this decision?"

Is your child able to see the results of both good and poor decision-making? Can your child generate good options in the face of impulsive group situations?

Associating with others away from the family for extended periods of time, seeking independence with less adult supervision, and seeking comfort from the approval of friends are all hallmarks of adolescence. If my teen displays the ability to keep herself safe in increasingly independent situations, I feel correspondingly secure about adding more time away from their direct supervision. My trust with her has been built from previous good decision-making. Providing emotional tools to guide my child to a feeling of safety for herself apart from me is foundational to her successful independence.

Feeling and keeping herself safe is not only a function of behavior. Emotional safety is key as well. Knowing and acting on intuitive feelings when feeling emotionally unsafe requires a teen to perceptively read another's intent, then judge whether that person is acting in good faith and with her best interest in mind.

We all fear that our exploring teen will submit to the thinking of friends who are unable to assess risk and exhibit poor decision-making in independent situations. Making sure your teen understands you are always there to assure her safety requires acceptance and teaching, not punishment.

Unfortunately, there are those who see their role of parent as a sculptor. They hammer and chisel at their children to become what they want them to be rather than raise them in the way they are bent.

It's our job to be the gardener and not the sculptor of our children.

We know a dad who was a doctor and expected his sons and daughter to follow in his footsteps. When his children were in high school, he spent millions of dollars building an office building he openly declared was built so his children could office with him when they became doctors.

None of them became doctors. And interestingly enough, they all moved as far away from their father as they could without leaving the country.

This dad was trying to be a sculptor, not a gardener. When we fail to accept and recognize our children's uniqueness and God-given purpose, they become afraid to show us who they really are. They will either spend their lives reluctantly and miserably bearing the burden of expectation we place on them or they'll reject us altogether and go their own way.

Every child has their own God-given bent. As parents, we have the amazing privilege of discovering their uniqueness and nurturing them.

When our children feel a sense of emotional safety, they aren't afraid to show us who they really are.

Touch and Sensory Stimulation

As children move into the teen years, parents sometimes back off and feel awkward showing physical affection to their teenager. And many teens don't like to show affection to their parents in public. But this is a time of life where physical affection is crucial. Teens need to know what healthy touch looks like, since they're bombarded with mixed messages from culture. The need for healthy touch is so deep that teens will seek it out one way or another.

This, too, is a biological shift that takes place in the brain of a young teen. God has created us so the brain of a child shifts in a way as to thrust young teens out of the nest, so to speak. This separation from their families of origin prepares them to venture out to begin a family of their own.

You may sense your teen pulling away in certain ways, which is healthy. It is important to keep in mind that pulling away doesn't mean a total disconnect. A subtle pulling away is healthy. A total disconnect is not.

As teens go through this biological shift, they often don't understand it themselves. They know something has changed, and there may be a great deal of emotional turmoil brewing below the surface. Your child may suddenly avoid the goodnight embrace or pull back to a less intrusive form of touch, such as a hand on the shoulder or a pat on the forearm.

This stage of development is marked by such extreme physical growth and sexual maturation. Teens are increasingly aware of both sexual desires and their own and others' awareness of physical development. Due to the increased peer influences of this age, discussion of family values and how others think, feel, and behave will help your child to think critically. Your guidance in regard to issues of sexuality requires open discussion.

A girl needs to spend time with Dad so she has a healthy picture of how she should expect to be treated and to know what healthy boundaries are in regard to touch. Playful touch continues to be important. Rough-and-tumble play is still enjoyed by many teens, but it may become more challenging for Dad to win!

Adolescence is a pivotal time in a young girl's development. She needs her dad more than ever to be a part of her life and model a relationship of respect and love. Conversely, boys benefit from a mother's direction for a healthy picture of how to treat girls with respect. Healthy boundaries need to be a continuing discussion regarding touch with both sexes, with an emphasis on the intersection of emotion and behavior.

Sometimes teens withdraw from being touched by parents because they don't feel lovable. The turmoil of the teen years can cause emotional tensions that can be interpreted as rejection. Small moments of affectionate touch can communicate volumes as teens navigate these unknown waters.

Other areas of sensory communication with teens are important as well. Eye contact can help a parent discern how a teen is feeling or whether words match behavior. An exchange of glances can communicate caring, unity or concern. Movement such as walking/running together, family hikes, dancing, rocking, or any rhythmic activity done together cements the experience in a manner other than words.

Sensory information is the first way in which we communicated with our children—through touch, singing, rocking, eye contact, and feeding. These methods continue to connect us in a primitive manner that communicates a fulfillment of unspoken needs. Parents and children's experiences of nonverbal communication are some of our most powerful moments of connection because they link our past with our present.

Parents need to recall early rituals as adolescents and young adults love to hear about their early experiences. Storytelling has for generations been a means of returning to meaningful times and relaying the importance of shared experience. From my grandmother's "putting on my makeup," tickling my face in a soft and gentle manner, to leaving my six-year-old with my perfume on a cotton ball so she could "smell me" in my absence, early and revisited sensory stimulation is important to bridge connection.

Attunement to your Teen

To paraphrase Thomas Paine's famous quotation, "These are the times that test parent's souls." This is how many parents feel when their developing teen displays ever-changing moods and feelings. Providing a predictable environment that encourages settled thinking and focusing on the present are essential. Helping teens feel secure in the battle of adolescence and providing guidance for right decisions, can be difficult—but so rewarding as you observe their growing self-assurance!

Hearing our teens' feelings and reflecting them back with understanding of the pressures they may be feeling helps us stay attuned with one another. When we can offer a back rub or manicure, which can alleviate physical tension and stress, we show our teen the connection between physical relaxation and emotional comfort.

Sometimes, without direct eye contact, we can help them relax and become more open to express their feelings. It's why our children will often talk more openly to us in the car when the focus is elsewhere.

Secure and connected relationships offer us all, children and adults, the security of intimacy that helps us feel both understood and validated.

- *Taking a sigh of relief with a parent who understands in a nonjudgmental manner how hard a test was restores a teen's balance.*

- *Having your mom give a reassuring hug and share her experience of feeling inferior to others, when a friend has chosen to hang out with friends other than you supports feelings and offers hope.*

- *Losing a big soccer game and having Dad offer comfort, validation of your performance, and share in your disappointment provides security of self-worth.*

With continued displays of support from a caring parent, teens start to feel an internal sense of control and a clearer sense of meaning, allowing them to venture out with increased confidence.

The critical interactions that developed our trust as an infant, gave us increasing certainty in our voice as a toddler, helped us make things happen as a school-age child, and created our growing ability to see cause and effect, are the same ingredients revisited as a teen. When parents maintain a playful attitude that communicates pleasure in relationship with their teen, they supply the motivation that engages their confidence.

The reinforcement of trust during the teen years is vital as the teen branches out to depend on increasing relationships outside the family. Open communication serves as a basis for checking in and helps parents and teens to stay attuned as life becomes more complex. When a teen begins a part-time job—and builds trust with others—you have an opportunity to help her feel prepared and confident in a new experience.

Guiding your teen by openly hearing his voice, allowing him to speak his piece, and validating the worth of his opinion (even when we may not agree) allows us to be attuned to the teen's developing sense of self. Parents often feel if the child is compliant or does not openly disagree, there are no problems within the relationship. This is not the case. When a parent is accepting of the teen's right to respectfully disagree and teaches them how to communicate disagreement, the parent–child relationship can withstand differences of opinion without relationship rupture.

When a teen's voice is silenced due to a parent's inability to hear differences of thought, the teen may begin to comply or manipulate—and the practice of respectful disagreement is lost. Hearing your teen's voice and opinion can be particularly hard for parents when the focus of their opinions, questions, and exploration leads them to disagree with strongly held beliefs, such as religion or politics. When a parent joins a child in their quest to answer questions and concerns, the child feels attuned, rather than feeling the need to control or withdraw.

As teens become more proficient in developing skills, the attuned parent will actively participate quickly and responsively to help promote those gains. Helping teens look at next steps and tracking their feelings allows for brainstorming options to roadblocks along the way. When you engage with your teen, their friends, and their important relationships outside your family, you help them learn the effects of their emotions and behaviors within the context of those relationships.

Normal teen relationships are marked by periods of peer approval or disapproval. If your teen is feeling left out or hurt from being excluded from activities or friendships, the ability to help read cues and retain stability through the rough spots can strengthen the parent–child relationship.

With my own teens and in my practice, I have watched young people feel alienated from friendships for numerous reasons ranging from academic snobbery to social exclusion. Teens can leave friendships abruptly, not having practiced how to start new relationships and incorporate others into an existing friend group. I've witnessed parents' social expectations adversely affect relationships between friends as teens grasp for an understanding of what is important in abiding friendships. These assessments of importance can change day to day, and a teen's self-worth can be swept about in the tempest of these moments. Not feeling "good enough" is a powerful deterrent for a teen's developing sense of identity.

This is an important time when parents may want to ply their child with reassurance and offer unlimited compliments in an effort to ease the hurt of a "friend's" evaluation. A parent's ability to help their child look at the reasons for another's cruel remarks, misguided judgments, or impulsive statements will help the teen learn to separate themselves from the words and behaviors of others. Guiding your teen by asking them questions that allow them to step back and think critically in these situations has lasting impact.

Are others' assessments of you (or others) made with the best interests of that person in mind?

Are comments or behaviors an attempt to "one up" another?

What might be some reasons people lash out or talk behind your back?

Are there any truths in what people say? And if so, how are they affecting your relationships?

A fifteen-year-old girl I counseled was emotionally overwhelmed by her friend's depression over her parent's domestic unrest and pending divorce. She was concerned her friend had begun to use street drugs to self-medicate the pain. Other peers at school were distancing themselves from this girl, talking about her behind her back as her behavior began to disintegrate. The pressure to keep her friend's secrets as her actions went further out of bounds had begun to wear on the friend who wanted to help but didn't want to betray confidences.

Helping her to separate her own feelings from the feelings of her troubled friend—and looking at what she could control—helped her to identify the needs of each person. She could control her honesty that the problem was beyond her means to intervene in order to get her friend the help she needed. She could support her friend with understanding, prayer, and efforts to seek adult support and access the right resources. She could stand up to others about the need to understand pain that others might not understand. She could demonstrate grace by modeling friendship for someone who others belittled.

Strong friendships are built from lifting others up and helping when they are in need. Guide your child on how to think independently. Help her to assess when situations are in her control—and when they are beyond her scope and require additional resources. Teach her to practice emotional intelligence, to identify and control her emotions, when friends may react to her hurtfully. Help her to be gentle with herself and others as she practices positive assertions of her developing skills and individuality.

While developing a strong sense of self, adolescents continue to have a strong need for parent's support and guidance. As they explore their own personhood, teens need these connections now more than ever. Begin and end each day with a connected experience.

* *Enjoy a special breakfast at your teen's favorite restaurant.*

* *Have a family picnic at a park, away from screens and other stimulation.*

* *End the day with a back rub after a hard day at school*

When children have been taught to seek God's plan for their lives, they begin to "connect the dots" of the occurrences in their lives. They don't see progress in their lives as coincidence or "luck," but as discernible guidance from the one who created them with a specific purpose.

Parents serve as the earthly guidance through which God can speak, when we seek His plan together.

Playful Engagement

Play remains an important component to maintaining strong emotional connections throughout childhood. The nature of the play changes as children get older, but taking time for play is crucial.

Play with teenagers may evolve into setting reliable times to be active with mutually shared interests like running, playing sports, working on projects or playing family games together. Because time with your adolescent decreases in the natural progression of their increased time with friends, school obligations, and extracurricular interests, carving out time together for planned activity will be important.

However, making yourself available for the spontaneous game of basketball or relaxing venture to have manicures together should take precedence over tasks that can wait until later.

Ignoring the invitations of our children or hijacking their interests to accommodate our own preferences undermines strong emotional connections.

It doesn't mean that we allow teens to use play as a way to manipulate us or avoid their responsibilities. If our teenager has agreed to do his homework before he plays catch with Dad, he needs to be held accountable to his agreement.

This also doesn't mean that we can't introduce our teen to new forms of play and different experiences. Part of our job as a parent is to issue invitations to try new activities and take advantage of new opportunities. But it means that we need to be attuned to their reactions and responses and maintain availability, offer coaching, and encourage.

Allowing our children to lead in play continues as well in the teen years. Look back to the experiences you enjoyed with the adults in your own life. Many will be around simple pleasures where laughter, shared experience, and affirmations of just being together were the key ingredients.

Tips to Remember

- Schedule family downtime to assure adequate rest, self-care, and foster connection (Sunday night game night, rotating menu selection, or cooking together).
- Introduce and share responsibility for table topics at dinner (identifying gratitude, discuss evolving thoughts regarding values, current events, and topical issues).
- Encourage increased responsibilities (assess abilities for initiative, capacity for critical thinking, and follow through).
- Identify family rituals that are enjoyable and create more time for them (encourage your teen's input into meaningful rituals).
- Maintain a teaching approach versus expectation of end results in accomplishing new behaviors (identify steps or resources to accomplish goals).
- Recognize timing in confrontation or "hard discussions" (Are you or your child tired, preoccupied, or emotional?).
- Request permission for expressions of opinion or ideas. ("I've got some thoughts about that. Would you like to hear them?")
- Utilize opportunities to model kindness, conflict resolution, or other teachable moments in your child's presence (with service personnel when orders are incorrect, patience in frustrating situations, aiding others when help is needed).
- Initiate discussions about what places teens at risk, and behaviors and emotions that may indicate depression or risk for suicide (sexual behaviors leading to pregnancy or sexually transmitted disease, behaviors contributing to unintentional injuries and

violence, unhealthy dietary behaviors, inadequate physical activity, and drug, alcohol, or tobacco use.

- Help your child understand societal and spiritual differences and honor culture through exposure to heritage events, developing appreciation for their—and others'—cultural and spiritual affiliations.

- Maintain active relationships with teachers, families, friends and others seeking assistance—and identify resources to be a part of solutions as a family.

Reflections

How do you offer support and encouragement to your teen that maintains your attachment?

What are some of the family rituals that all family members look forward to and participate in?

Chapter Eleven

Attachment through the Lifespan:
Enjoying Generational Relationships

Maintaining and strengthening emotional connections with our children is a lifelong journey. Even though we all have identifiable attachment patterns at one year of age, healthy connections need to be nurtured throughout life.

The good news is unhealthy forms of attachment can change, but it takes understanding and intentionality to repair early deficits.

Throughout childhood and the teen years, children continue to have the same basic needs as they did in infancy—they just manifest a little bit differently. Most of children's so-called "bad behavior" is often the result of unmet or misunderstood needs. Instruction and correction given in the context of unconditional love by a parent who models grace changes the hearts of children—not punishment or harsh discipline.

Parental selfishness and convenience can lead to children's challenging behaviors. Our culture wants parenting to be convenient and easy and all about us.

Parental selfishness can lead to children's challenging behaviors. Our culture wants parenting to be convenient and easy and all about us.

We are increasingly concerned about the callous parenting of those who consistently turn their children over to others for care and nurture. More and more parents look to substitute caregivers to provide the ingredients we've outlined, and are then surprised when their children are increasingly anxious and detached, and show little regard for others. And tragically, these moms and dads are heartbroken when the child leaves the nest and disconnects from them on all levels: physically, emotionally, and relationally.

It does not have to be this way in your family.

One of the greatest myths of our culture is, *we can have it all*. We'll say it again: "We *can* have it all, but not all at the same time." There are seasons of life. When we choose to have children, we are choosing them over our own aspirations, dreams, and personal goals.

What Is Our View of Our Children?

How does our view of children matter in daily life? What does our belief about the nature of children have to do with our parenting?

How we view and value our children affects how we care for them. Many parents are unaware of the importance of the infant's early life and development. They believe, as many do, that until they are verbal, they register little experience. This is the old "blank slate" belief that children can't remember early experiences.

Let's examine our beliefs and the consequences of those beliefs.

Infancy: If I view the infant who wakes up in the night as having done so as a willful act or evidence of his flawed character, then I will either ignore his needs or respond harshly. If I view the child through the lens of grace and as gift, I will respond with loving compassion and soothe the baby back to sleep no matter how inconvenient losing sleep is for me.

Toddler: If I view the "no" of a toddler as an act of willful defiance, I will respond with power and control with the intention of overpowering his will. But if I see the child through the lens of grace and as a gift, I will see his no as a declaration of independence and celebrate his growing autonomy.

This is where understanding of child development equips to you be a better parent because you understand the reason for behaviors in each stage. I would respond with empathy to his frustration and handle it with gentle redirection rather than harsh discipline or punishment.

166

Preschooler: If I view the preschooler who whines incessantly as a manipulative child, out to get his own way, then I will begin to feel like a victim myself, and may lash out in anger.

School-age: If I view the school-age child who sulks and balks at doing their homework as a lazy and unmotivated child, then I will respond with disgust and frustration. I may use coercive strategies such as taking away TV time, friend time, or allowance. But if I see the child's behavior as an indication of a lack of understanding or feelings of incompetence, then I will respond with support and find the help the child needs to be successful.

If I view teenagers as rebellious and self-centered, I will respond in controlling and antagonistic ways. But if I understand that the teen years as a period of time when the brain is going through significant change—and teens are re-evaluating their values and beliefs in order to establish their own framework for life—we will respond with patience and support.

Take some time to consider how you view your children. Is that view grounded in God's view of children or a misguided twisting of truth? Is it guided by your own convenience rather than a true understanding of the needs of children?

Nurturing Trust

Trust is the ultimate foundation upon which the parent-child relationship is built. Attachment and trust go hand in hand—they're really two sides of the same coin. Nurturing your child begins and ends in trust.

The child who has not learned to trust Mom and Dad will typically struggle to build a trusting relationship with God. Throughout the Scriptures, God invites us to trust Him. He desires that we live our lives leaning on His unconditional love and the fact that He has our best interest at heart. But in order to trust a God that cannot be seen, children must first learn to trust *people*.

Young children are very concrete thinkers and must experience abstract concepts in tangible ways. A child who lives with the confident expectation that their parent will always be there for them will typically find it easier to transfer the same trust to their relationship with God.

Trust is intended to be developed within the context of the home and family. This means that even your church cannot build the foundation of a relationship with God—this privilege is yours, and also that of older generations.

The beauty of trust is that it can be built—and re-built!

Relationship and attachment can be built—and re-built.

This includes the relationship with your children and your relationship with God. Yes, we're encouraging you to think and pray about your relationship with God.

Your family can grow and change. Partnering with God—and the hard work of honest self-reflection—helps us to think, feel, and behave differently. Our prayer for healing becomes, "Search me, O God, and know my heart; Try me and know my anxious thoughts; And see if there be any hurtful way in me, and lead me in the everlasting way" (Psalm 139:23–24).

The process of becoming more like Jesus often involves changing our own attachment pattern, to move from an insecure to secure attachment. This begins with making sense of our own story and how our past influences our present, especially in the relationships we have with our children.

We will continually be in the process of making sense of our story, so we can be fully present in the moment—and for the generation standing in front of us.

Too often, the root cause of rebellion and behavioral issues is identified as lack of strict punishment. By now, you know that's not the case.

Discipline Versus Punishment

Most parents associate discipline with punishment. But there's a big difference for you and your child!

The word *discipline* comes from the word *disciple*—someone who is a follower of the teachings of another. So let's ask ourselves, "Am I the kind of person I want my children to follow?"

If we look at the life of Chris, we see that He did not influence his followers by punishing people—He did it through these ways:

• Instruction

• Correction

• Coming alongside and modeling words and behavior

Children don't always listen well, but they are always watching and imitating us.

What's the most powerful tool for shaping behavior? Relationship.

My power to influence and lead my child is directly related to the strength of the relationship that I have with them. True discipline connects whereas punishment alienates.

Time outs, spankings, or taking things away are the most common forms of punishment that we hear moms talk about. But does punishment change behavior, or is there a better way to think about this?

Why do we think we can make children do good by making them feel bad?

Consequences vs. Punishment

Traditional approaches to parenting basically start with the underlying notion that making children feel bad will somehow make them want to do good.

"Time out" is an example and probably one of the most popular forms of punishment. This assumes that children engage in inappropriate behavior because they choose to, and that isolation and separation will make them want to change.

What is wrong with spanking? It teaches children that power and pain dominate. I want you to be "nice," so I hit you. That doesn't make sense and undermines the fundamental role of the parent as a child's protective shield.

When children feel threatened, they are biologically driven to seek safety and protection from those who love and care for them. But when those who love and care for them are the source of the fear, the child has nowhere to do go. It is psychological poison.

Think back to our relationship with God. The more we love Him the more we want to please and obey—and deepen our relationship.

A consequence is the result or effect of an action or condition. All of our behaviors, attitudes, and actions have a consequence—positive or negative. The consequence for studying for an exam is increased likelihood that I will pass it. The consequence of pulling the cat's tail is that the cat will likely scratch me.

Children should always be held accountable for their actions in a way that informs and teaches them the appropriate thing to do, through demonstration, modeling, coaching and practice.

Tools for the Tool Box

If we let go of punitive forms of discipline, what do we do instead?

One of the simplest, and most effective, changes parents can make is instead of time out, giving a "do-over." But we must make sure that the child really knows what the appropriate behavior looks like.

You might have to give your child the words to say. For example, you are sitting at the dinner table and the child demands, "Gimme more potatoes!"

Say something like, "Let's try that again. This is what we say: 'May I have more potatoes please?'" Then have the child say the words and model the tone.

There is a scientific principle at work here. When a child does a "do-over" we're actually activating the connections in the child's brain related to appropriate behavior. If we consistently respond and ask the child to "try it again," each time we do that, the connections in the brain are becoming more established and the child is more likely to demonstrate appropriate behavior.

When you child grabs a toy from a sibling say something like, "It's not okay to grab toys from other people. Here's what you say, 'May I please have a turn with the truck?'" Then require that your child repeat the words.

The child with the truck is likely to say, "No, I'm not done." Just because a child asks appropriately doesn't mean he is entitled to receive. When this happens, give the child additional words to say. "When you are finished with the truck will you let me know so I can have a turn?"

After the child says these words you will probably have to give the child a "waiting strategy." Otherwise, he is likely to hover over the other child, bugging him to hand it over. You might say something like, "While you are waiting would you like to play with Legos or make something with the clay?"

This type of modeling and do-over is helpful to children of *all* ages.

Another strategy is "ignore the 'no' and give two yeses." When your child pushes back to a request and says, "No," ignore the no and follow up with two opportunities for a "yes." If your child says "no" when it's time to go to bed, respond with, "would you like to hop like a bunny or have a piggy back ride?"

This kind of response assumes obedience but shares power with the child. I am in control without being controlling.

Role playing difficult scenarios with your child is also a way of establishing appropriate behaviors. If your kindergartener gets in trouble for pushing a child after someone grabs the ball he is playing with, act out the appropriate response at home. You might use stuffed animals, action figures, or role play with brothers and sisters.

Rigidity is often an issue and gets in the way of good parenting. Flexibility, problem solving, and reason are tools we use as children get older.

Accountability is always appropriate. Shame is not. Holding children accountable for their actions builds strong kids with grit. Shaming and punishing them pushes them into rebellion. Letting them get away with bad behavior makes them weak.

We won't always get it right—it's not about being perfect but being authentic.

We are going to mess up. But modeling the process of owning your own mistakes, and making it right, allows children to realize that relationships don't fall apart when someone doesn't get it right.

Modeling "I'm sorry" is a strong example for your child. When we can acknowledge our mistakes, telling a child your frustrations got the better of you, or letting a child know when they were right and you were wrong, teaches that mistakes can be made and quickly corrected.

It is vitally important for children to see adults take responsibility for their behavior. It's also important for children to have a community of attachment relationships with adults from every generation.

Generations of Healthy Attachment

As a society, we are losing important connections with older relatives. In previous generations, attachments included grandparents and older friends who served as guiding lights for various seasons of life. Our children benefit from living illustrations of long-term relationships, and how playful engagements are demonstrated through the years.

The wisdom and example of how to weather challenges, live with losses and changes, and how children and grandparents stay attuned with the difference in generations, are all important lessons for children.

It is crucial for children to have a community of attachment relationships with adults from every generation.

Being the youngest of eighteen grandchildren, with eight aunts and uncles, my cousins and I (Cathy), were surrounded by a Native American family. We practiced faith together, had frequent family reunions, and celebrated one another's accomplishments, while also mourning each other's losses. Relatives were always available to sit through surgeries with waiting family, provide food and childcare for periods of stressful seasons of life. We playfully engaged in ways that left us yearning for more.

The safety of this extended network was a real and present protection that I've carried throughout my life. Hugs abound, tears are shed together, and words of encouragement are always found amidst this safety net of attachments. Each additional generation is brought into the fold of loving care and given a protective identity.

The benefits of *layers* of secure attachments have protective benefits to health, physical and emotional security, and personal well-being. You can't buy this kind of healthcare because it's free. The cost is a lifetime of loving investments—caring for one another and faithfully abiding while treating one another as "we'd like to be treated."

Simple. Yet requiring daily commitment. It is the same in our relationship with our Creator. Responding to His grace, patience, and loving guidance of our lives, our attachment is intact, secure, and guaranteed.

We are all valuable children of an accessible and protective God.

Take time to see yourself in your Heavenly Father's eyes.

Acknowledgements

In our practices of working with families and children, as throughout our lives, we have been drawn to appreciate beginnings in relationships, realizing their importance for trust and hope thereafter.

We are grateful to God who created us for relationship; our husbands, Bob and Marc, who inspire and motivate us; and our daughters: Krista, Ashley, Sara and Carly, whose laughter, strength and connection mirror our hopes for love's possibilities.

ENDNOTES

Chapter 1

Thompson, Curt (2010). *Anatomy of the soul.* Carol Stream, Ill.: Tyndale House.

The Birth Injury Guide (2018). Retrieved April 2018 from www.birthinjuryguide.org.

Chapter 2

Perry, B. & Szalavitz, M. (2010). *Born for love.* New York: Harper and Row.

Field, T., Diego, M. & Henandez-Reif, M. (2010). Preterm infant massage research: A review. Infant Behavior Development 33 (22) 115-124.

Leach, P. (2018). *Transforming infant well-being.* New York: Routledge Press.

Lieberman, A. & Van Horn, P. (2008). *Psychotherapy with infants and young children.* New York: NY: The Guilford Press.

Chapter 3

Shore, A. (2003). *Affect dysregulation and disorders of the self.* New York: W.W. Norton and Company, Inc.

Chapter 5

McClure, Vimala (1979) *Infant massage: A handbook for loving parents.* New York: Bantam, 2000

Chapter 6

Chess, S. & Thomas, A. (1986). *Temperament in clinical practices.* New York: NY: The Guilford Press.

Chess, S. &. Thomas A. (1999). *Goodness of fit: Clinical applications from infancy through adult life.* Philadelphia: Bruner/Mazel.

Chapter. 7

Lieberman, A. & Van Horn, P. (2008). *Psychotherapy with infants and young children*. New York: NY: The Guilford Press.

Gopnik, A. "Theories and illusions." *Behavioral and Brain Sciences,* vol. 16, no. 1, 1993, pp. 90-100.

Gopnik, A. (2017). *The gardener and the carpenter: What the new science of child development tells us about the relationship between parents and children.* New York: Farrar, Straus and Giroux.

Kardaras, N. (2016). *Glow kids: How screen addiction is hijacking our kids—and how to break the trance.* New York: St. Martin's Press

Fellitti, V. *The adverse childhood experiences study.* Keynote address. Annual Zero to Three Conference. Washington D. C. December 2011.

Thompson, Curt (2010). *Anatomy of the soul.* Carol Stream, Ill.: Tyndale House.

Chapter 8

Benzer, S. (1971) From the gene to behavior. JAMA, Nov. 15:218(7):1015-22.

Colin, V. (1991) *Infant Attachment: What We Now Know.* Prepared for U.S. Department of Health & Human Services, Nancy Low & Associates, Inc.

Chapter 9

Lieberman, A. & Van Horn, P. (2008). *Psychotherapy with infants and young children.* New York: Guilford Press.

Martin, S. (2006). *Thy rod and thy staff they comfort me.* New York: Sorensic Press.

Webb, W. (2011). *Corporal punishment and the bible.* Downers Grove, Ill: Intervarsity Press.

Ingram, C. *The biblical approach to spanking.* (2006). Retrieved February 2018 from https://www.focusonthefamily.com/parenting/effective-biblical-discipline/effective-child-discipline/effective-child-discipline

Chapter 10

Siegel, D. (2013) *Brainstorm: The teenage brain from the inside out.* Brunswick, Vic.: Scribe Publications, 2014.

CDC: Centers for Disease Control, Parent Information, A-Z, Teens (Ages 12-19)-Risk Behaviors.   (September 6, 2015) Retrieved from https://www.cdc.gov/parents/teens/risk_behavior

About Dr. Barbara Sorrels

Barbara Sorrels, EdD was initially educated in the field of child development and later pursued continuing education in neuroscience, with an emphasis of the effects of trauma on children. She gathered her experience through four decades of work in churches, running child care centers, teaching primary school, as well as teaching at the university level.

She consults with the legal system on behalf of children. and has completed NMT training certification through the Phase I level with The Child Trauma Academy, founded by Bruce Perry, M.D., Ph.D.

With her neuroscience training, Barbara now directs and leads a small developmental preschool, and consults on the subject of trauma in children: training parents, teachers, and professionals around the country.

Along with her daughter, Barbara hosts a popular podcast for parents. She has authored two books: *Reaching and Teaching Children Exposed to Trauma; and Ready or Not Here Comes School.* She and her husband are proud parents and grandparents.

www.DrBarbaraSorrels.com

About Cathy Chalmers, MA, LPC, NCC, LMFT

Cathy Chalmers, MA, began her career working in the first psychiatric treatment center for children and adolescents in the U.S., leading her to specific work with families, adoption, attachment, and permanency placement. She helped cofound an international organization, ATTACh, Association for Training on Trauma in the Attachment for Children, also providing therapy in a developmental pediatric clinic. Cathy currently conducts adoption home studies and works in the legal system, securing permanency placements for children, tackling the complex issues of placements of Native children.

Cathy has worked in the field of adoption, attachment, and family therapy for nearly 40 years as a therapist, trainer, and home study provider. She is a qualified expert witness in child development, attachment & adoption, and testifies in court regarding best interests and the Indian Child Welfare Act. She holds a bachelor's degree in psychology from Oklahoma State University, master's degree in Educational Psychology from University of Nebraska-Lincoln, and is a Licensed Professional Counselor, Nationally Certified Counselor, and Licensed Marital and Family Therapist.

www.CathyChalmers.com

Thank you!

We hope this book has been helpful to you and your family.

Please share this message with expectant moms, parents, and children's ministry leaders at your church.

Barbara and Cathy are also available to do seminars on parenting, adoption, foster care, and workshops on the effects of trauma on children.

For new resources and encouragement, please subscribe for email updates here:

www.DrBarbaraSorrels.com

Continuing education, resources in your state, and an ongoing parent support group are available through www.ATTACh.org

Cheering you on,

Barbara and Cathy

Made in the USA
San Bernardino, CA
06 March 2019